Contents

Illustrations by
E. Ratcliffe, E. A. Hodges
S. Livesey, A. Linsdell & S. Aspey

Edited by Mae Broadley

Copyright © MCMLXXI by
World Distributors (Manchester) Limited
All rights reserved throughout the world

Published in Great Britain by
World Distributors (Manchester) Limited
P.O. Box 111, 12 Lever Street, Manchester M60 1TS

Printed and bound in England by
Jarrold & Sons Ltd, Norwich

SBN 7235 0099 1

65p

13/-

ONCE A GREEN VALLEY

*A legend from Switzerland
retold by Katherine M. McLean*

Long, long ago, it is said that there was no ice or snow in Switzerland, except on the highest tips of the seven peaks which seemed to keep watch over the luxuriant valley far below.

At harvest-time the trees hung heavy with golden peaches and apricots; the hillsides became patches of green and purple where grape clusters covered the vines, and the meadows were fields of shining corn which sang and whispered with every passing breeze.

The soil in this valley was so fertile that little work would have been necessary except for one thing— *there was no water!*

No stream or river ran through the rich valley and it could not have been so fruitful had not one man, long before this story opened, cut a channel where there was sufficient water for all who would carry it away!

So every drop needed by the thirsty soil had to be carried laboriously, day in, day out, through all the growing seasons.

Even so, you would have thought that the people would count this small payment for a reward so great as the abundant harvests.

But no!

Everyone grumbled as they toiled to and fro with their pails of water.

"Why wasn't the channel cut nearer?" was a constant cry.

"Work—work—work——" a man grumbled, putting down his pail and rubbing his hands before setting off once more. "The channel should have been cut nearer to *my* vines——"

"*Your* vines," snorted a youth, angrily. "What about my peaches?"

"Why don't you take the water to them instead of dawdling here?" asked an old man, sitting on a boulder.

"What's the good of arguing?" asked a youth, coming up to the little group and overhearing the last words. "The water isn't near to any of us and we must all carry our share.

Look at my hands—calloused with the never-ending business of carrying heavy pails. What do *you* say, old man?"

The old man smiled, wrinkling up his tanned face with the effort.

He looked at the speaker.

"What do I think?" he said. "I think of a land flowing with milk and honey——"

"We don't want milk and honey," said a young girl pertly, as she joined the group with her friends. Their water pails clattered on the stones and their laughter greeted her sally. "We'd be better off with water—and more men to get it, instead of standing about gossiping."

The old man ignored the interruption.

". . . where no man need raise a hand. I dream of our vineyards blossoming and fruiting—aye, without any hard work from me!" He chuckled.

The girls laughed.

". . . and you'd have us sit in the sun all day with nothing to do?" asked one. "That wouldn't suit me at all," she added, with a toss of her head.

"*I'd* not sit in the sun," cackled the old man, "I'd be off to the big town having a good time with the money I hadn't earned! There are lights and sights to see in big towns—and beautiful girls——"

A youth grinned at the old man's fancy. "They'd not look at you, old man," he jeered. "Fill your bucket or you'll not have enough grapes to sell even in the smallest village. . . . Thinking like that won't bring you wealth!"

"We'd better be on our way," suggested an older man. "Come along, let us pick up our buckets."

And, one by one, or in twos and threes, they went for the precious water which would be swallowed up by the rich earth.

There was silence, except for the singing of birds. And then an old man, rather oddly dressed, stepped from the sheltering bushes where he had stood, listening to the chatter of the villagers.

He wore a long cloak which completely enveloped him; on his straggly grey hair perched a round cap; his long beard looked as shabby as his clothes.

He walked about, touching a peach here, an apricot there, marvelling at the fine quality of the fruit.

"What harvests!" he muttered. "Great ripe figs hanging like purple lanterns; peaches as golden as glass balls. So beautiful a land—and all the people can do is grumble!"

He watched the men and girls staggering along with heavy pails, the water dripping over the edges and spilling like so many diamonds.

"I have never seen such crops," he said as a man came near.

The man started.

"How satisfied you must be," went on the stranger.

"Satisfied?" grunted the man. "You must be a stranger here or you'd know that we have no time for anything but work. Satisfied, indeed!"

He turned to the others who, glad of an excuse to put down their buckets, joined the two men.

"Our aches and pains don't give us any satisfaction," said the old man. "I'm old. What pleasures have I had in my life?"

"But surely——" began the stranger.

"We know what you're going to say," interrupted a youth, "but we're tired of the endless work—

carry — carry — carry — year after year, toiling endlessly up the valley from one miserable wooden channel of water, pail after pail. Why shouldn't we have water as other people have?"

There was angry muttering, and agreement, and above it all rang the complaint: "Why can't we have water?"

The stranger held up his hand and, oddly enough, the muttering died.

"You may have water—if you wish," said the stranger.

The crowd goggled.

"We may have it? Have water? Who are you?" they cried, as they crowded round him.

"Are you a magician?" cried one.

"You may call me that," smiled the stranger. "I can certainly tell you how to get plenty of water if you want it."

Again there was a loud outcry.

"Want it? Want water? Of course we want water."

"Go on, stranger, tell us how we may get water," said one, bolder than the rest.

"If he knows!" jeered a girl.

"Aye, if he knows!"

The man held up a silencing hand, and again the people quietened.

"You will choose seven of your most beautiful maidens." Once more a look from this strange man hushed their opening cries of protest. "Each must climb one of your seven peaks," continued the stranger, "to the land of eternal snows. Each must dig out a lump of ice——"

The crowd looked puzzled.

"What then?" asked one, boldly.

"Each must plant the lump of ice at the head of your valley."

At this there was an outburst of mocking laughter.

"And *that* will give us seven pails of water," cackled the oldest villager. "Ice and snow melt! Our maidens must climb peaks such as men have never trod to collect seven pails of ice!"

"Seven pails of water for our orchards," squealed one of the girls. "I'd rather go to the channel—it's nearer!"

Everyone laughed.

"You will have water enough if

you do as I say," said the stranger.

"If it could be so!" sighed another, almost convinced.

"I believe he means it!"

Excitement seized the crowd. Their voices rose shrilly: "Water for our crops! Water for our fruits! No more toiling." They danced about, chanting their hopes: "Time to go to the towns!"

"New gowns!"

"New machinery for my farm."

Then they quietened and looked about at their maidens—they were all beautiful—it should not be hard to pick out seven!

The stranger broke in on their thoughts.

"But take care that the great white cow does not devour your valley," he warned them.

The girls giggled. What white cow was this?

"Why, he means the mountain peak!" said a young girl. "I'd chance that. I'll climb a peak——"

Again the stranger interrupted: "I have warned you. Before you rate ease and pleasure above hard work and rich harvests, remember my words. Farewell."

Quite suddenly—he had gone!

"Silly old man," shouted someone, with mock bravado.

"Do you think he *was* a wizard?" whispered another, fearfully.

"I'll climb a peak, wizard or not!" shrilled a girl.

"Who says you're the prettiest?" shouted her companion.

Then came the squabbling. Weren't all the maidens beautiful? Who was to choose seven from among them?

But, at last, this was done. Seven maidens set off towards the eternal snows, through fields of waving corn, through orchards . . . up . . . up . . . until at last they reached the snow caps!

The blocks of ice were cut, the return journey made.

What jubilation filled the valley!

With shouts of joy the ice blocks were planted at the head of their valley.

And then . . .

The blocks grew . . . grew . . . GREW . . . to become a great glacier which crept slowly, relentlessly, along the once fertile valley.

The white cow had devoured the green meadows and left the valley in a grip of ice.

IT'S ALL in a word

Have you ever tried to learn French, or German, or maybe Italian? If you have, just think how difficult it is for a Frenchman, or a German, or an Italian to learn English. After several years' study he can no doubt manage the grammar and the pronunciation. But he is still quite baffled by some of our strange phrases and idioms. *You* take them for granted, and use them every day; but do you ever think where they have come from? You may be surprised!

LOSING THE SHIP FOR A HAP'ORTH OF TAR

This phrase doesn't apply to a ship at all! It refers to a sheep—which was commonly pronounced 'ship' by rustic villagers. Sheep used to be marked with their owner's initials in hot tar, and if an unmarked sheep was lost and couldn't be claimed back, it had been lost for the want of a hap'orth of tar.

GOING ON HONEYMOON

There was an ancient custom in some European countries for a newly-married couple to drink metheglin, mead or hydromel—drinks made from honey—for thirty days after their marriage. This is how we get our term 'honeymoon', or 'honeymonth'.

SPICK AND SPAN

Cloth used to be taken from the loom and laid out on spikes (hooks) and span-nans (stretchers) so that it was all stretched equally. A piece of cloth just taken from the stretchers was called 'spick and span new', and this is the most likely explanation of how we came to use the phrase.

Some people believe that it comes from the Italian word 'spicco', which means 'brightness', and the English 'span new'—newly span or spun. And there is also a theory that it comes from the Dutch 'spyker', a warehouse, and 'spange', glossy or shining.

HE'S A BRICK

If someone goes out of his way to help us over something, or is especially kind, we sometimes say, "He's a brick."

This quaint expression comes from an incident in Plutarch's writings about the life of Agesilaus (King of Sparta). An ambassador once visited Agesilaus on a diplomatic mission, and was shown over the capital. The ambassador knew that the monarch was very powerful, and he expected to see massive walls and towers for the defence of the towns. But there were none.

Puzzled, he asked Agesilaus why this was so. The following day Agesilaus led his guest out on to the plains, where his huge army was assembled. He pointed to it proudly and said, "These are the walls of Sparta—10,000 men, and every man a brick."

APPLE-PIE ORDER

There are so many theories about the derivation of this phrase that everyone has become rather puzzled. Here are just three possible explanations—perhaps you can think of one, too!

An old cookery book contains a recipe for a Devonshire squab pie, made out of 'alternate layers of sliced pippins and mutton steaks', arranged in the most orderly manner.

And there is a children's story which begins "A was an apple pie; B bit it; C cut it; D divided it". If this is the true derivation 'apple-pie order' refers to the regularity of the alphabet, always A before B, B before C, and so on.

The third suggestion is thought to be the most likely. It used to be the custom to take the top crust off an apple-pie, mix sugar and cream into the fruit, cut the crust into triangular pieces, and stick them into the fruit in various patterns, circles, crosses, stars, or more ingenious designs.

Any of these explanations could be the right one—or you may have heard another which sounds more likely. Think about it next time you are getting your handbag or your school desk into apple-pie order!

ROBBING PETER TO PAY PAUL

The Abbey Church of St. Peter, Westminster, was raised to the dignity of a cathedral on December 17th, 1540. But ten years later it was joined to the Diocese of London again, and some of its wealth was taken for repairs to St. Paul's Cathedral.

Some people believe that a great deal of the land of the Abbey was appropriated by great men of the Court, and that they tried to cover up for themselves by giving a small part of the spoil towards the work at St. Paul's.

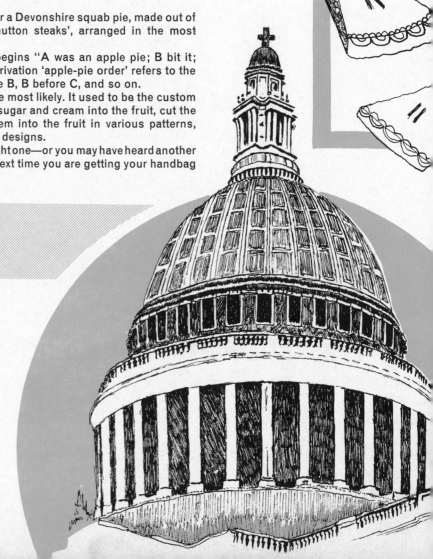

BY HOOK OR BY CROOK

This is another phrase which has many possible derivations, and there is only rather vague evidence to support any of them.

One explanation is that in days of old the poor of a manor were allowed to go into the forests "with their hooks and their crooks" to get wood. If they could not reach the wood with their hooks they could pull it down with their crooks.

Another theory is that after the Great Fire of London in 1666 boundary-marks of different properties were confused, and two clever lawyers named Hook and Crook were generally chosen for court proceedings as authorities on the subject. So a debate about a boundary might well end "We must get it settled by Hook or by Crook."

The people of Waterford in Ireland claim that when their country was invaded by Strongbow (in the time of Henry II) he decided to land at Hook Head or Crook Point, saying that he would conquer Ireland "by Hook or by Crook".

HOBSON'S CHOICE

It may sound rather odd, but we use this expression when we mean that we have no choice at all! One possible derivation is that it refers to a livery-stable keeper called Hobson who would only let out his horses in strict rotation. So if you hired a horse from him Hobson's choice would have to be your choice too!

Finding out the derivations of words and phrases like this is a fascinating hobby, and it's also very amusing to think of possible explanations for yourself. Have fun—in a word!

11

✳ Stranger than Fiction ✳

THE *TOUCAN'S* BILL, THOUGH VERY HUGE AND POWERFUL, IS VERY THIN AND WEIGHS ALMOST *NOTHING*

WESTMINSTER ABBEY IS NOT *REALLY* AN ABBEY. IT IS OFFICIALLY CALLED THE *COLLEGIATE CHURCH* OF *ST. PETER*

QUEEN ELIZABETH SENT HER MARINERS ALL OVER THE WORLD, YET SHE NEVER EVEN LEFT ENGLAND. HER LONGEST JOURNEY WAS 112 MILES TO BRISTOL

THE *SPARROW* GETS ITS NAME FROM THE *ANGLO-SAXON* WORD *SPEARWA*, MEANING 'FLUTTERER'

WHITE, AND NOT *BLACK,* IS THE CORRECT WEAR AT *CHINESE FUNERALS*

IN THE 18th CENTURY WHEN WOMEN'S HAIRSTYLES WERE *TALL* AND *COMPLICATED* THEY HAD TO STAY UP FOR *LONG PERIODS* FREQUENTLY THEY BECAME *INFESTED* WITH *MICE,* AND AT NIGHT THE *LADIES* WOULD *SLEEP* WITH TINY *MOUSETRAPS* BESIDE THEIR *BEDS*

WOLFGANG AMADEUS *MOZART* (1756-1791), THE *AUSTRIAN COMPOSER,* WAS AN EXTRA-ORDINARILY PRECOCIOUS CHILD. HE *BEGAN PLAYING THE CLAVIER* AT THE *AGE* OF *THREE* AND WAS *COMPOSING* AT *FIVE.* AT *SIX* HE *TOURED EUROPE* AS *PIANIST* WITH HIS *TEN YEAR OLD SISTER*

HIGH BORN CHINESE DID NOT GROW NAILS LONG JUST FOR APPEARANCE BUT TO SHOW THAT THEY WERE *INCAPABLE* OF *MANUAL WORK*

Swing along Scarf & Beret

Protect yourself from the winter's icy blasts by making this neat beret and maxi-muffler in crochet. The snug-fitting beret will certainly keep your head warm, and if you make the scarf long enough it might even keep those draughts off your knees too!

Materials: Of Patons Ninepin Midi-Knitting in Old Gold 293. *Beret:* 4 (1 oz.) balls. *Scarf:* 16 (1 oz.) balls. Nos. 9 and 10 crochet hooks.

Measurements: *Scarf:* width 13 ins., length 66 ins. (excluding fringe). *Beret:* to fit average hat size.

Tension: 9 sts. and 7 rows measured over 2 ins. in pattern using No. 9 hook.

Abbreviations ch.=chain; s.s.=slip stitch; y.o.h.=yarn over hook; d.c.= double crochet; tr.=treble; Cl.= cluster, worked as follows:—(y.o.h.,

insert hook through back of work round cluster made 2 rows below, and draw loops to same length as tr. just worked) 4 times, y.o.h. and draw through all loops on hook, 1 ch.

SCARF

With No. 9 hook, make 60 ch. **Next row:** 1 d.c. in 2nd ch. from hook, 1 d.c. in each following ch., 59 sts., turn with 3 ch.

Next row: 1 tr. in 2nd st. from hook, (y.o.h., insert hook in next st. and draw

loops through) 4 times y.o.h., and draw through all loops on hook, 1 ch., * 1 tr. in each of next 5 sts., (y.o.h., insert hook in next st. and draw loop through) 4 times, y.o.h. and draw through all loops on hook, 1 ch.; rep. from * to last 2 sts., 1 tr. in each of last 2 sts. Continue in pattern as follows:

1st row: wrong side facing, 1 d.c. in each of next 2 sts., * miss 1 st. (ch. of previous row), 1 d.c. in each of next 6 sts.; rep. from * to last 3 sts., miss 1 st., 1 d.c. in each of next 2 sts., 1 d.c. in top of turning ch., turn with 3 ch.

2nd row: 1 tr. in 2nd st. from hook, 1 Cl., miss st. behind Cl., * 1 tr. in each of next 5 sts., 1 Cl., miss st. behind Cl.; rep. from * to last 2 sts., 1 tr. in each of last 2 sts.

These 2 rows form pattern. Rep. them until scarf measures approximately 66 ins., ending with 1st pattern row. Fasten off.

Work 1 row d.c. along side edges. Press lightly on wrong side under a damp cloth.

Cut remaining yarn into 6-inch lengths and taking 6 strands together each time, knot through short edges to form a fringe.

BERET

With No. 9 hook, make 4 ch. and join into a ring with s.s. **1st round:** 6 d.c. into ring. **2nd round:** 2 d.c. in each d.c.: 12 sts. **3rd round:** * 2 d.c. in 1st st., 1 d.c. in next st.; rep. from * to end: 18 sts.

4th round: 2 ch., * 2 tr. in 1st st., 1 tr. in next st.; rep. from * to last 2 sts., 2 tr. in each of last 2 sts.: 28 sts.; join with s.s. to top of 2 ch.

5th round: 2 ch., * 1 tr. in 1st st., (y.o.h., insert hook in next st. and draw loop through) 4 times, y.o.h. and draw through all loops on hook, 1 ch.; rep. from * to end, join with s.s. to top of 2 ch.

6th round: 1 d.c. in each st.: 42 sts.

7th round: 2 ch., * 1 tr. in each of next 2 sts., 1 Cl., miss st. behind Cl.; rep. from * to end, join with s.s. to top of 2 ch. **8th round:** as 6th: 56 sts.

9th round: 2 ch., * 1 tr. in each of next 3 sts., 1 Cl., miss st. behind Cl.; rep. from * to end, join with s.s. to top of 2 ch. **10th round:** as 6th: 70 sts.

11th round: 2 ch., * 1 tr. in each of next 4 sts., 1 Cl., miss st. behind Cl.; rep. from * to end, join with s.s. to top of 2 ch.

12th round: as 6th: 84 sts. **13th round:** 2 ch., * 1 tr. in each of next 5 sts., 1 Cl., miss st. behind Cl.; rep. from * to end, join with s.s. to top of 2 ch. **14th round:** as 6th: 98 sts.

15th round: 2 ch., * 1 tr. in each of next 6 sts., 1 Cl., miss st. behind Cl.; rep. from * to end, join with s.s. to top of 2 ch. **16th round:** as 6th: 112 sts.

17th round: 2 ch., * 1 tr. in each of next 3 sts., (y.o.h., insert hook in next st. and draw loop through) 4 times, y.o.h. and draw loop through all sts. on hook, 1 ch., 1 tr. in each of next 3 sts., 1 Cl. miss st. behind Cl.; rep. from * to end, join with s.s. to top of 2 ch.

18th round: as 6th: 140 sts. **19th round:** as 11th. **20th round:** as 6th: 168 sts. **21st round:** as 13th. **22nd round:** as 6th: 196 sts. **23rd round:** as 15th.

24th round: * 1 d.c. in each of next 7 sts., miss 1 st.; rep. from * to end.

25th round: as 23rd. **26th round:** * 1 d.c. in each of next 3 sts., miss 1 st.; rep. from * to end: 168 sts. **27th round:** as 13th.

28th round: * 1 d.c. in each of next 3 sts., miss 1 st., 1 d.c. in each of next 2 sts., miss 1 st.; rep. from * to end: 140 sts. **29th round:** as 11th. **30th round:** * 1 d.c. in each of next 2 sts., miss 1 st.; rep. from * to end: 112 sts. **31st round:** as 9th.

32nd round: * 1 d.c. in each of next 4 sts., miss 1 st.; rep. from * to end.

33rd round: as 24th: 98 sts. Change to No. 10 hook and work 6 rounds d.c. Fasten off. Press lightly on wrong side under a damp cloth.

Peggy Pigtails

A Girl Guide story by K. McGarry

The football came soaring over the railings of the city park, and landed at the feet of two passing Girl Guides. It bounced twice. Then with a sudden loud hiss it subsided into a shapeless mass of leather.

Marty Dean bent to pick it up. She had to be careful not to squash the cakebox she was carrying. As she straightened up, her companion Kitty Brett said with a chuckle: "Someone has kicked the stuffing out of that."

Kitty was a plump, jolly girl with red hair that was always unruly, and now stuck out in twists and curls from under her blue beret.

Both girls were in the same patrol, the Honesty Patrol, and Kitty was the leader. She was carrying a carrier-bag loaded with tins of food, and a Christmas pudding.

"What shall I do with it? Throw it back?" enquired Marty.

Her friend shrugged. "I suppose so. I can hear some boys yelling. . . . Oh, here's one of them climbing through the railings."

They watched as a slim figure in blue jeans, football boots, and a very tattered sweater came squirming through the railings.

"Is this your ball?" asked Marty, as the other tugged his peaked cap into place and turned towards them.

"Yes, it is. . . . Oh, lor! What happened?" The voice was that of a girl with a long, lively face. She stared in dismay at the deflated football.

"It must have popped," explained Marty, staring at the other girl's tomboy appearance.

"It went down just as it hit the ground," added Kitty.

The girl snatched off her cap and slammed it on the pavement in a fit of bad temper. "Just my luck!" she stormed. "Now the perishin' team will never let me play in their perishin' games."

The two Guides were startled, and not a little embarrassed by such childish behaviour. They stared at the girl. She wore her lank brown hair in plaits, and now that her cap was off they fell from their hiding-place.

Marty found her voice first. "You mean that you play with the boys?" she asked.

"'Course I do!" The tone was scornful, and the ice-blue eyes surveyed the Guide in a pitying way. "It's only boys what play footer, ain't it?" she asked.

There was a crashing in the bushes. Several boys peered through the railings. One, in a leather coat, shouted: "Come on, Piggy! Let's get on with the game."

The girl hurriedly jammed the cap back on her head. But this time she forgot to hide her pigtails, and they hung down her back. She held out the burst ball. "It's busted. I must've kicked it too hard. . . . But I'll get it fixed," she said.

The boys looked at each other. "Aw, come on, gang," said a fat boy with long hair. "Let's go riding on our bikes."

The girl they had called Piggy said anxiously: "What about the match on Saturday then?"

Another boy said: "What match? No ball, no match! Remember?"

Piggy was almost begging them, as she said: "I'll get it fixed—honest I will! Just promise I can play against the Mafeking Street team."

The boys seemed to enjoy her discomfiture. They grinned. Then leather-jacket spotted her pigtails. "Smashin' centre-forward you'll be, wiv pigtails hangin' down," he scoffed. Then he began to lead the rest in a derisive chant: "Piggy Pigtails! Piggy Pigtails!"

The gang scrambled away through the bushes, still chanting. Marty saw tears welling up in the ice-blue eyes. Then the girl's face screwed up in another flash of temper. She snatched off her cap, and seemed ready to hurl it on the ground again. But she caught sight of the Guides' curious gaze, and changed her mind.

"Boys!" she gritted scornfully. "They're horrible."

"Then why play with them?" reasoned Kitty.

The girl gave her an impatient look. "I like to play football, that's why," she snapped.

Kitty felt a bit offended. She was about to suggest that they'd better be getting along, when Marty said: "Look, I gather they've made it a bargain that if you supply the ball you can play football with them. Right?"

The girl nodded. "Okay," went on the Guide. "Then mend the puncture, or get a new bladder, and you're all right."

The other kicked the railings with her football boot. "Oh, that's no good. I wouldn't know how to begin to put a new bladder in."

Marty smiled patiently. "Well, look—er, what's your name?"

"Peggy," said the girl.

"Well, if you want to get a new bladder, we'll put it in for you," promised Marty.

Peggy's eyes lit up. "Honest?"

Kitty laughed. "We put new bladders in our netballs all the time," she said. "We've got the tool for lacing it, as well as the pump and the adaptor."

"It's jolly good—I mean, it ain't arf kind of you," burst out Peggy. She peered curiously at their uniforms. "You Girl Guides?"

"That's right," nodded Marty. She introduced herself and Kitty, and went on: "Do you live round here, Peggy?"

A guarded expression came into the girl's eyes. "Er—no. But my aunty does. I'm stoppin' with 'er."

"Then maybe you could help us," said Marty. "We're delivering some food to a couple of old people who live round here. It's part of our Troop's Christmas effort."

Peggy took the scrap of paper with addresses on it that Marty had produced. She looked at it and nodded. "I can show you where these places are. And while you're deliverin' the stuff, I can go and get a football bladder and fetch it to this last address."

"Right," said Kitty. "Ask for a size four."

The three set off down the road. Marty was encouraging this

strange new friend to talk about her love of football. She had never imagined that any girl could be so keen on a boy's game. . . . Besides, there was something mysterious about Peggy.

"She tries to seem so tough," Marty explained to her friend later. "But I think it's all an act. And she seems to be *trying* to talk as common as she can."

When she had led the Guides to a street of shabby houses due for demolition, and pointed out the houses they wanted, Peggy ran off down the street. Her football boots clattered, and she whistled through her teeth.

"What a tomboy!" chuckled Kitty.

"She certainly works hard to *seem* like one," replied Marty cryptically, as she knocked on the first door. . . .

With the burst football under her arm, the tomboy went quickly to the nearest sports shop. She came out with the new bladder and the case wrapped in a neat parcel.

At the street corner she paused. From the back pocket of her jeans she took a gold wristwatch. Her eyes widened as she saw the time. "Oh, jimminy!" she murmured. "I'm going to be late home."

She hurried back into the area of shabby old houses. A back entry took her to the gate of the backyard of one of the houses that was neatly painted. She let herself in and clattered up the stone flags. The door of the house opened, and an old lady looked out: "That you, Miss Elizabeth?" she called.

"Yes, Anna," called the girl.

"Then you'd best look slippy or you'll be missing that train to Budleigh," said Anna.

The girl hurried into a tiny scullery. A kettle was bubbling cheerfully on the range. Like her house, Anna was old, but trim and neat. She wagged her head and clicked her tongue in disapproval as Peggy put down her parcel and tossed her hat on to a hook before struggling out of the ragged sweater.

"Dearie me! I don't know as it's right, what we're helping you to do," sighed Anna. She reached for the teapot and warmed it from the kettle.

And now when Peggy spoke, the roughness in her speech was gone. "Oh, please, Anna," she begged as she wriggled out of her stained jeans, and scrambled into a smart skirt and blouse. "I know it's not right of me to use you and Ben like this. But *do* try and understand. I'm just crazy to play football, and there's no other way I can get in a team."

Anna sniffed sadly as she made the tea and began to slice bread. "Ah. . . . And that's all Ben's fault, too. Fancy him teachin' you to play football while he was your gardener down at Budleigh. . . . He ought to have had more sense!"

Peggy stopped fastening on her watch. "But I *wanted* him to teach me. I *asked* him," she said. "And, after all, he was such a well-known player himself when he was young."

Anna paused as she loaded a tray

with tea things. There was a faraway look in her eyes as she said: "Ay . . . he was that . . . when he had his health."

Then she bustled into the back room of the little house. "She's come at last, Dad," she said, as she set the table.

Peggy came bouncing in, and threw her arms round the neck of an old man, crippled with arthritis, who sat in a chair by the gas fire. "Hello, Ben," she greeted him.

He peered at her fondly. "Did you have a good game? Did you get plenty of practice?"

"Yes—until the ball burst," said Peggy, and went on to describe what had happened.

Ben looked sadly at his own twisted hands and said: "I could 'ave put that new bladder in your ball like a shot, if it wasn't for this pesky ailment."

"Never mind," said Peggy, as she sat at the table and began to eat. "I'll get the little boy next door to take it to the Guides, and ask them to meet Peggy Pigtails with the ball on Saturday."

Anna came bustling towards the girl. "That reminds me," she exclaimed. "Your hair! You can't go home with pigtails. Now finish your tea, and I'll brush it out."

Peggy obeyed. And as she ate, and had her hair brushed out, she listened to Ben talking football tactics.

A few minutes later she left the house, looking very neat in a red coat and white tam-o'-shanter, and hurried towards the station, carrying a music case.

The last liquid notes of a Brahms prelude floated from the Bechstein grand piano. They hung, quivering, in the large oak-panelled room. Mrs. de Vere Cheevers rose from the antique chair in which she was sitting. She was a very stately person, dressed with sober but exquisite taste. She nodded approvingly at the young girl seated at the piano. "Very good, Elizabeth. I must say that these extra Saturday lessons you've been having in town seem to have been well worth while."

"Thank you, Aunt Bertha," said Peggy Pigtails—for it was she.

Her aunt glided gracefully towards the piano. "Yes, I think you are quite ready for your first public performance," she declared.

Peggy tried to hide the dismay she felt. "Oh, no, Aunt Bertha, I—I——"

She might have saved her breath.

"Now, Elizabeth, no need to feel bashful," said the other.

"But I just can't play the piano in public," protested Peggy.

A steely glint came into the woman's grey eyes. "Don't be ungrateful, child. You know that ever since your parents died and you came to live with me I have done everything to foster your musical talent—with a view to you one day going on the concert platform."

Peggy gave up resisting. She knew how iron-willed her aunt could be. "Where is it you want me to play?" she asked quietly.

The grey eyes grew kinder. "It's a little concert arranged by Lady Backby in Backby Hall. It's part of a fund-raising campaign for a Youth Centre and sports ground for Backby Village."

"A sports ground?" Peggy stood up, suddenly interested. "You mean —for football?"

Her aunt waved impatiently. "Oh, I don't know. . . . Yes, I suppose so. I think those village lads have a sort of team called the Hornets."

"A *sort* of team!" burst out Peggy, forgetting herself. "Why, the Hornets won the county youth cup."

"Really!" said Aunt Bertha dryly. She turned away, uninterested. "Well, I'll go and call Lady Backby and tell her what you'll be playing. She wants to make up the pro- gramme," she said.

When the night of the concert arrived, the guests who arrived at Backby Hall for the concert were shown to their seats in the Banquet Hall by smiling Girl Guides, who also sold programmes.

After the concert began, they stood at the back waiting to serve refreshments.

First there was a baritone, and then a troupe of Morris Dancers.

After that, Lady Backby, who was compering the concert, announced "a young lady who is quite a child prodigy at the pianoforte . . . Miss Elizabeth de Vere Cheevers."

The prodigy walked to the grand piano, to a ripple of polite applause.

Marty Dean, one of the Guides, nudged her friend Kitty. "Haven't we seen her somewhere recently, Kit?" she whispered.

The patrol leader looked puzzled. "I can't remember . . . But I know what you mean. There's something so familiar about her face. . . ."

"Ssh-sh!" A woman turned and glared fiercely.

The Guides forgot to puzzle over that long, lively face, as the girl bent over the keyboard. Instead they

marvelled at her playing. Her long fingers moved crisply over the keys, and Marty noticed that she wore a ring on the little finger of her left hand.

Elizabeth de Vere Cheevers was the hit of the concert. The audience called her back for an encore. They were still applauding as she left the hall, smiling and bowing.

And once more something began to nag Marty's brain. That piquant face, and those determined eyes. . . .

On Saturday morning Marty and Kitty were waiting near the city park with the mended football. Soon they saw the tomboy figure of Peggy Pigtails running towards them. She ran with big, boyish strides, her football boots making a clatter, and she had on the same blue jeans, tattered sweater and peaked cap as before.

"Did you get my ball fixed?" she shouted.

Marty held out the ball. "Yes, here you are."

"Oh, thanks." The girl held out her hands to take the ball. In a flash, Marty's keen eyes had noted the white circular mark on the little finger, from which a ring had been recently removed.

"We thought you were marvellous, playing the piano," said Marty. She spoke on impulse, but watching the other's face she knew she had scored a bull's-eye.

For a moment Peggy looked as if she was going to cry. Then she bit her lip, and stood staring at the football.

"Are you *really* Elizabeth de Vere Cheevers?" asked Kitty.

Peggy shrugged resignedly. "Yes. But I wish I wasn't." She spoke bitterly. "What fun d'you think

ALL CLUED UP

How high do you rate your knowledge of fashion and beauty? Try this simple quiz to assess your knowledge.

1. Heads turned on a Sydney racecourse when an English model walked by. Who was the girl and why did she cause such a stir?

2. Which well-known vegetable can also be used as a skin toner and astringent?

3. *Coco* is the title of a musical based on the life story of a famous Paris fashion designer. Who was she?

4. We usually only think of wearing silk stockings. Can you think of any other uses for them?

5. Who designed the first dresses to be made entirely of plastic discs?

6. What are freckles?

7. Who designs the tennis dresses for the female competitors at Wimbledon?

8. Can you give the names of the three most popular dress lengths of the 1970s?

9. By what name is Lesley Hornby best known?

10. Who was the originator of the 'New Look' of the late 1940s?

11. What is the name of the famous London street said to be the centre of the London fashion scene for the young?

12. Which famous fashion designer is married to Alexander Plunket Greene?

ANSWERS

1. *Jean Shrimpton, sometimes known as the 'Shrimp'. She wore a mini dress, modest by British standards, but never seen before in Australia.*

2. *Cucumber. Slices rubbed into the skin after cleansing help to reduce oil on greasy skins and tone normal skins.*

3. *Coco Chanel. Her perfume, Chanel No. 5, is one of the most famous in the world.*

4. *If you put a silk stocking over your hair-brush when brushing your hair the silk polishes your hair, making it shiny and healthy looking.*

5. *Paco Rabanne. His first dresses in 1967 consisted solely of linked squares of plastic or leather.*

6. *Freckles are due to the anti-sunburn pigment melanin being distributed over the skin in clumps instead of an even film. When the sun hits these clumps they darken rapidly and form freckles. Skin which has an even distribution of melanin darkens gradually and does not form freckles.*

7. *Teddy Tinling, who brought frills to the tennis courts and who stages a fashion show every year before Wimbledon.*

8. *Mini—from 3 inches above the knee. Midi—mid calf length. Maxi—ankle to floor length.*

9. *Twiggy, who became the most famous fashion model of the late 1960s.*

10. *Christian Dior, perhaps the most famous fashion designer in Paris.*

11. *Carnaby Street, a whole street full of boutiques.*

12. *Mary Quant, who revolutionised the British fashion scene with her new ideas, and who was awarded the OBE.*

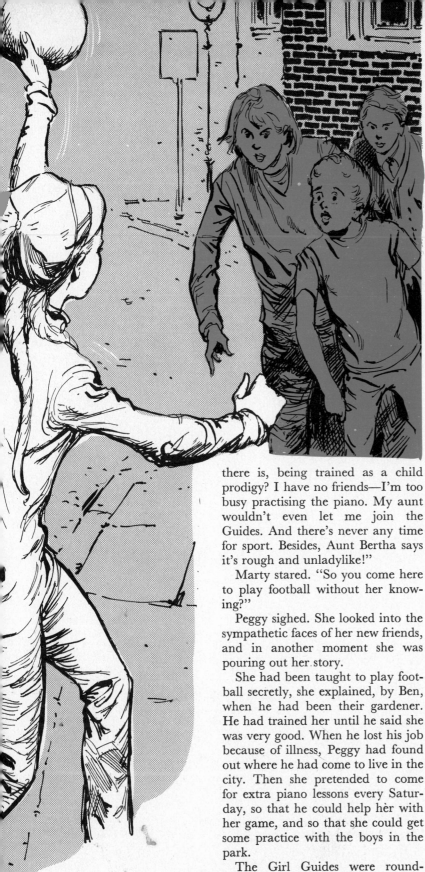

"I'd be scared of getting knocked about," admitted Marty. "The things I see on 'Match of the Day' make me shiver!"

Peggy bounced the ball and balanced it skilfully on her instep, before tossing it back into her hands. "Ben has taught me how to play without getting hurt," she said. "I don't think it's so tough."

"But you have to *act* tough with these city boys, I notice," said Kitty.

Peggy nodded. "Oh, yes," she agreed. "It wasn't easy to get a game with them at first. But when they found out how well I could play. . . ."

She broke off as a piercing whistle rang out above the noise of the traffic. The girls turned to see a group of boys standing at the park gates.

"Hey, Piggy! Got your ball?" yelled one.

Peggy held up the football. It was obvious that the boys were very relieved.

"Well, come on! We've got to play the Mafeking Street team," shouted another.

Peggy yelled: "Orright! Wait a tick, can't you!" Then she turned towards the Guides. "Will you keep it a secret?" she asked quietly.

Both answered in one voice: "Of course!" And Marty added: "Can we come and watch you play now?"

The tomboy tugged her cap to a rakish angle and winked. "Orright, come on," she chirped.

The football pitch was badly worn by the games of countless children. In patches, the white lines that had marked the pitch could not be seen. The goalposts were huge steel affairs, built to withstand the gymnastics of energetic teenagers.

As for the two teams—well, neither Marty nor Kitty had ever seen such oddly assorted players. There were long, stringy boys and short, tubby boys; some with football shirts, some with football boots, and all rather tough and fearsome.

The Mafeking Street team were jeering and shouting at Peggy, who was at centre-forward. But once the game got under way they were forced to change their tune. Every time Peggy got the ball the Mafeking defence came under pressure.

there is, being trained as a child prodigy? I have no friends—I'm too busy practising the piano. My aunt wouldn't even let me join the Guides. And there's never any time for sport. Besides, Aunt Bertha says it's rough and unladylike!"

Marty stared. "So you come here to play football without her knowing?"

Peggy sighed. She looked into the sympathetic faces of her new friends, and in another moment she was pouring out her story.

She had been taught to play football secretly, she explained, by Ben, when he had been their gardener. He had trained her until he said she was very good. When he lost his job because of illness, Peggy had found out where he had come to live in the city. Then she pretended to come for extra piano lessons every Saturday, so that he could help her with her game, and so that she could get some practice with the boys in the park.

The Girl Guides were round-mouthed and round-eyed with wonder when Peggy finished.

"You *must* be keen on football!" said Kitty admiringly.

Suddenly, a loose ball landed between her and a beefy opponent. He made a hefty lunge—but Peggy was there first. She foxed the other boy, and went jinking away through the defence. Two of them closed in from opposite sides, but Peggy changed her direction with a lightning swerve. At top speed she accelerated towards the goal. Out rushed the gangling youth, who seemed to be all arms and legs. Peggy let him come, shifting the ball from left foot to right, and tantalising the goalie until he flung himself forward. In that instant Peggy let rip with a right-foot shot that zipped between the goalposts.

"Oh, she's marvellous!" gasped Kitty.

"Hurrah! Good old Peggy!" yelled Marty.

"Aw, she was just plain lucky," claimed a long-haired youth standing nearby.

But that proved far from true. Luck had very little to do with the dazzling performance that Peggy put on. There was assurance and skill in every move she made. Not that she sought self-glory. She was constantly feeding the ball to her fellow forwards, running fleet-foot here and there, and covering a tremendous amount of ground as she sparked off one attack after another.

Her second goal came in the second half of the game. The left winger had outrun the full-back, and centred with a ball that drifted plumb into the goalmouth. Before anyone could move there was a flash of green and blue and Peggy had nodded the ball into the goal.

"Oh, great!" exclaimed Kitty.

"Yes, very good indeed," came a deep voice behind them.

A man in a fur-trimmed car-coat stood watching the game. "Who is that girl who's playing?" he wanted to know.

Marty said cautiously: "Why do you want to know?"

"Well, my name's Joe Killigan. I'm assistant manager of the City team," said the man. "They've asked me to round up a team of city boys to play against a team of Backy Village. It's for their fund-raising campaign."

Marty and Kitty exchanged quick glances. "You mean your boys' team will play against the Hornets?" asked Kitty.

Killigan nodded and grinned. "Are you both fans of the Hornets?" he wondered.

"Well, not exactly," said Marty. "But we live out Backby way, and we're very interested in the fund for the Youth Centre."

"Yes, and I'm sure you'll find Peggy interested, too," added Kitty.

'But would you *really* ask her to play?"

"I would!" Killigan spoke decisively. "A girl she may be, but I've yet to see a centre-forward to equal her."

After the game had ended, Killigan called several of the players to ask them if they would play in the charity match.

Peggy was glowing with excitement to find herself among those selected. But when she heard that the match against the Hornets would be played at Backby, a look of dismay came over her face.

When Killigan noticed her hesitation, he said: "Oh, don't let me down, Peggy! I need a centre-forward like you."

"Well, I—I——" Peggy broke off, finding it hard to put her refusal into words.

Marty had a sudden idea. "Why don't you use Peggy as a sort of gimmick, Mr. Killigan?" she asked. "I mean, having a girl on the team is unusual enough, but if you had a *masked* girl——" She left the idea to hang in the air.

Killigan was the first to speak. With a slow grin he looked at Peggy. "Now, that's quite a good publicity idea," he agreed. "Would you appear as the masked girl, Peggy?"

Relief showed in the tomboy's face. "Oh, I don't mind," she agreed.

Killigan brightened. "Fine! Then give me your shirt size and boots size, and I'll get your gear together during the week," he said. "We'll train every night at the City football ground. Five o'clock sharp. . . . See you later, boys—and girl!"

The Guides walked out of the park gates with a rather worried Peggy. "How am I going to manage to attend the practice sessions?" she wondered.

Kitty said: "Well, the schools are closed next week for the Christmas holiday, and some of our Guides are spending a few days at our cottage in the Lake District. Couldn't we ask your aunt to let you go?"

Marty caught on to the idea quickly. "Yes, only you needn't go, really. You can sleep with Kitty and I in our club hut at Backby. There's bunks in it, and a smashing stove."

"And we could come in for the practice sessions with you every night," added Kitty.

Peggy looked at her new friends with gratitude. "It's awfully good of you. Only—well, it means you'll have to tell lies—and that's not fair."

"Only little white lies," said Marty cheerfully. "After all, it's in a good cause—the new football ground and Youth Centre!"

Somehow the plan worked. What made Mrs. de Vere Cheevers relax her usual strict rules about her niece and agree to the idea of her spending a few days in the Guide cottage was a mystery. Perhaps she felt that Elizabeth needed the company of other girls of her own age; perhaps it was Marty and Kitty, smart as

new pins in their uniforms, and with manners to match, who inspired her with a new confidence. . . . At any rate she agreed to the Lake District trip.

Joe Killigan was well pleased with the way his boys' team was shaping. "At this rate, I think we can guarantee to give the Hornets a good run for their money," he told them, the night before the match. "Now, there's just one thing—I'll need all your names for the programme. So what are we going to call you, Peggy?"

She shrugged. "Well, since I'm going to be masked, it doesn't really matter what I'm called, does it?" she suggested.

"Why don't you put her down as 'Peggy Pigtails'?" said Kitty.

It was obvious that the Hornets regarded the whole thing as a joke when they took to the field against the city boys next day. When their opponents came trotting on to the field with the masked girl in their ranks, the village players raised a hoot of laughter.

Peggy paid no attention, and neither did her team-mates, who knew that an unpleasant surprise lay in store for the scoffers.

The Hornets kicked off. When the whistle shrilled, they bustled into the attack. It was obvious that they expected to make mincemeat of the visiting team. They stroked the ball about with almost contemptuous ease.

For a while the city defenders dithered as the Hornet strikers cut inside for the penalty area. Only Jumbo Jones, their right-back, showed any fire. A quick dart and he had the ball away from his man.

Hopefully be belted a long pass up the centre of the field. Peggy was after it in a flash.

The Hornet full-backs, fully committed to attack, were caught napping. They pelted back, but Peggy's speed kept her well in the lead. The ball danced at her feet as she sped on. The delighted spectators raised a chant of: "Go on, Peggy Pigtails!"

Only the goalie remained to be beaten. A strapping youngster, every inch six-foot-two, he came charging out to quell this audacious invasion. Peggy waited until her opponent was four feet away, then she flicked the ball neatly over his head. He made a grab—but it was too late.

"GOAL!"

The roar sent the crows flapping in alarm from the elm trees, as Peggy stabbed the ball into the net.

For the rest of that game the city boys played like a team inspired. Calmly and unhurriedly they took

apart the Hornets' defence. Attac after attack was led by Peggy.

A loose pass was snapped up b Ginger Stubbs, the centre-half. H loped down the field, then back heeled it to the inside-right as a ebullient Hornet forward made murderous rush at him.

The inside-right cut in confidently Then he seemed to hesitate, looking around him. It was an old dodge guaranteed to draw several defender to him. And it worked. As a wall o green jerseys closed around him, h laid his pass right at the feet o Chuck McGee, the winger, chasing unmarked towards the corner-flag.

Chuck steadied himself, and took careful aim.

Wham! The ball came zipping across the goalmouth. And ther from nowhere came Peggy, in a headlong dive, to turn the bal neatly into the net.

Hornets came back fighting, to score one goal in the second half But there was no holding the city players. Murdoch made it three with an impudent flick from twenty yards And even Jumbo came upfield to ge in on the act with an unstoppable drive from a corner-kick.

The crowd flocked on to the pitch as the final whistle went. Peggy found herself thumped affectionately by scores of hands, and jostled until she almost lost her balance. Someone tried to pull off her mask, no doubt wanting a souvenir.

When at last the two Girl Guides rescued the masked marvel and hurried her away to the Guide hut, Peggy was close to tears. . . .

"But aren't you thrilled?" exclaimed Marty, as they helped her to shed her disguise as Peggy Pigtails. "You were a sensation."

Peggy sighed. "I've done what I always wanted to do," she admitted. "But I'm not sure I like being a football star. I just like playing football!"

The two Guides exchanged secretly amused glances. "Oh, well," said Marty, as she brushed out the pigtails into the shining tresses of Elizabeth de Vere Cheevers, "I guess that, between the football pitch and the grand piano, you'll give 'em all a good run for their money!"

Let's go DANISH and have a party

A party with a Danish flavour is lots of fun not only to give but also to prepare. The secret is that the food is simple and nourishing, but that does not mean it's dull—most certainly not! The Danes go to town with their garnishes, they are both exciting and colourful.

Turning a nourishing and simple open sandwich into a mouth-watering buffet snack which will tempt every appetite is an art, but not one which is difficult to learn. The first step is to learn how to garnish.

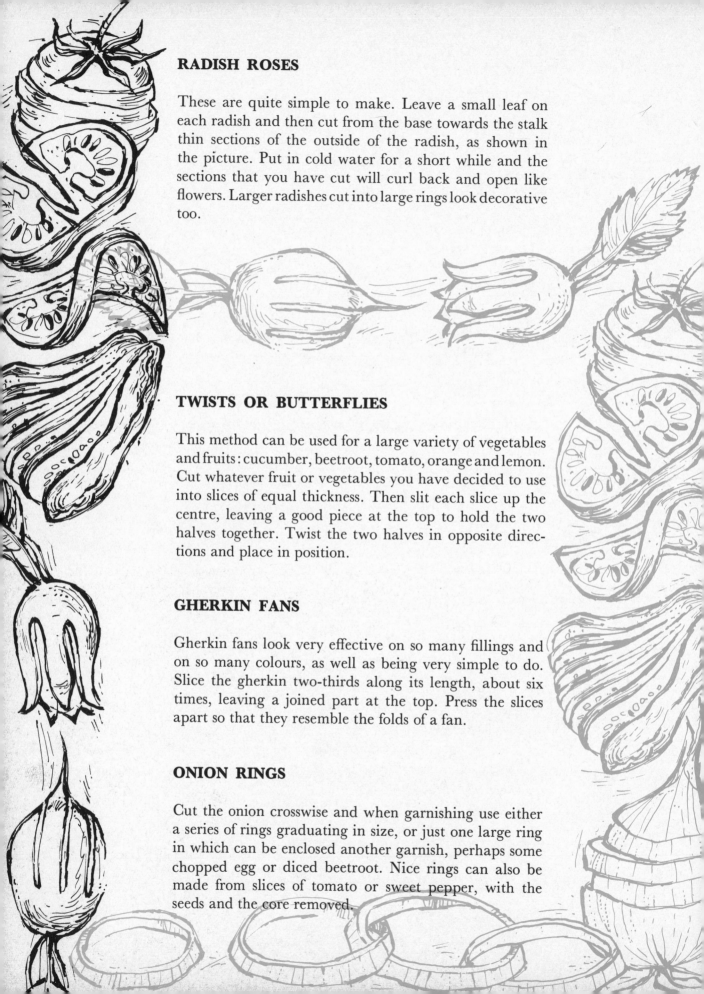

RADISH ROSES

These are quite simple to make. Leave a small leaf on each radish and then cut from the base towards the stalk thin sections of the outside of the radish, as shown in the picture. Put in cold water for a short while and the sections that you have cut will curl back and open like flowers. Larger radishes cut into large rings look decorative too.

TWISTS OR BUTTERFLIES

This method can be used for a large variety of vegetables and fruits: cucumber, beetroot, tomato, orange and lemon. Cut whatever fruit or vegetables you have decided to use into slices of equal thickness. Then slit each slice up the centre, leaving a good piece at the top to hold the two halves together. Twist the two halves in opposite directions and place in position.

GHERKIN FANS

Gherkin fans look very effective on so many fillings and on so many colours, as well as being very simple to do. Slice the gherkin two-thirds along its length, about six times, leaving a joined part at the top. Press the slices apart so that they resemble the folds of a fan.

ONION RINGS

Cut the onion crosswise and when garnishing use either a series of rings graduating in size, or just one large ring in which can be enclosed another garnish, perhaps some chopped egg or diced beetroot. Nice rings can also be made from slices of tomato or sweet pepper, with the seeds and the core removed.

DANWICH DELIGHTS

Using your new-found knowledge of garnishes it will be quite an easy matter to make all kinds of sandwiches, but I have included a few ideas here that you might like to try.

THE MILLER'S CHOICE

This open sandwich is made with Samsoe cheese, made on the island of windmills from which the cheese takes its name.

INGREDIENTS

3 slices Samsoe cheese
1 radish rose
Danish buttered bread

Danish bread is soft and tasty and is usually obtainable from most bakery departments. Spread thickly with Danish butter. The Danes consider bread poorly buttered if they cannot see their teeth-marks in the butter after taking a bite of their danwich! Lay the cheese on top and decorate with a radish rose.

ESROM DANWICH

Another Danish cheese is used for this open sandwich. This time it is Esrom, which has a nice full flavour and lots of tiny holes.

Tuck a piece of lettuce on one corner of the buttered bread and place the slices of cheese on top. Garnish each slice with a piece of stuffed olive.

INGREDIENTS

3 slices Esrom cheese
1 stuffed olive (sliced)
lettuce leaf
Danish buttered bread

THE CONTINENTAL

For this danwich use the king of spicy sausages, salami. It comes plain—if salami can ever be called that—or slightly flavoured with garlic, or for the gourmets amongst you, flavoured with rum or honey!

INGREDIENTS

4 thin slices salami
4 thin onion rings
lettuce
parsley
Danish buttered bread

Place lettuce on one corner of the buttered bread. Fold salami loosely in half and arrange in a fan shape on top. Make an onion chain by snipping through two of the onion rings and then link them together over the salami slices. Finish off with a sprig of parsley.

The Continental.

PICNIC DANWICH

Although this gay open sandwich is an ideal picnic-mate it is also an ideal party-goer.

INGREDIENTS

1 frankfurter sausage
slices of new potato turned in mayonnaise
1 radish rose
1 rasher of crispy bacon
lettuce
Danish buttered bread

Place the lettuce at one end of the buttered bread and then add the potato salad. Slice the frankfurter lengthwise and place on top. Garnish with the bacon and radish rose.

SHRIMP CRUSH

A Danish favourite, this danwich will delight everyone.

INGREDIENTS

1½ oz. shrimps (fresh or tinned)
½ oz. mayonnaise
1 lemon butterfly
lettuce
parsley
Danish buttered bread

Place the lettuce on one corner of the bread. Pipe a thin line of mayonnaise down the centre of the bread to hold your shrimps in place. Drain the shrimps well and pile them neatly and attractively on top of the bread. Pipe another thin line of mayonnaise down the centre of the shrimps and garnish with the lemon butterfly and parsley.

FOR THE SWEET-TOOTHED ONES!

To be complete your party table must have at least one or two sweet things. Two simple ones to try are Danish Apple Cake and Lace Biscuits.

LACE BISCUITS

INGREDIENTS

4 oz. Danish butter
4 oz. granulated sugar
4 oz. medium oatmeal
pinch salt

flavouring:
few drops of vanilla essence **or**
¼ level teaspoon ground ginger **or**
finely grated rind of half a lemon

This tempting danwich is called "The Epicure". A lettuce base is a delightful contrast to the golden fried chicken piece.

Cream the butter and sugar till light and soft. Stir in oatmeal and flavouring. Blend to a fairly stiff mixture and then roll the dough into small balls. Place on a greased baking-tray, leaving a good space between each. Bake on the centre shelf of the oven, 475°F (Mark 7), for 8 to 10 minutes, until golden brown round the edges. Leave to cool slightly and then remove to a wire rack. Serve plain, or sandwiched together with butter icing of the same flavour as the biscuits.

DANISH APPLE CAKE

INGREDIENTS

2 lb. cooking apples
1½ oz. Danish butter
caster sugar to taste
4 cloves
piece of lemon rind
stale 1 lb. white loaf (2–3 days old)
Danish butter for frying

to decorate:
whipped cream
chopped nuts

Peel, core and slice the apples and cook in melted butter, with sugar, cloves and lemon rind, until they are soft, but not mushy. Do not add water, but stir frequently to prevent burning. Leave to cool.

Remove crust from loaf and make crumbs; if the bread is too new, dry in the oven for a few minutes. Fry a few tablespoons of crumbs at a time in melted butter and then leave

This Danish Apple cake is all sweetness and light. Topped with fresh cream and chopped nuts, it's a perfect dessert.

to cool.

Put alternate layers of apple and crumbs in a dish, starting with apple and finishing with crumbs. Serve chilled, decorated with cream and chopped nuts.

By this time your party table should be groaning under the weight of all this delicious food, and I should think that you won't be able to resist holidaying in Denmark if you get the chance—if only for the food!

CENTREPIECE

Every party table needs a bright centrepiece, round which the rest of the food can be arranged. Why not have a cheese-board as your centrepiece, crowned with a Samsoe Sputnik!

Using a large orange as your base, cut a slice off the bottom so that it will stand firm and place on your cheeseboard. Cut 6 oz. of Samsoe into ¾ in. cubes and place one of these on the end of a cocktail-stick. Add a black or green grape, mandarin orange segment, or piece of pineapple to each cube of cheese, or use two pieces of different fruits for a really colourful effect. Push the other end of the cocktail-stick into the orange to form your sputnik. Round this, on the cheese-board, arrange your different Danish cheeses; Danablu, Esrom, Danbo, Emmenthaler and Maribo are just a few. Decorate with frosted grapes, orange segments, etc.

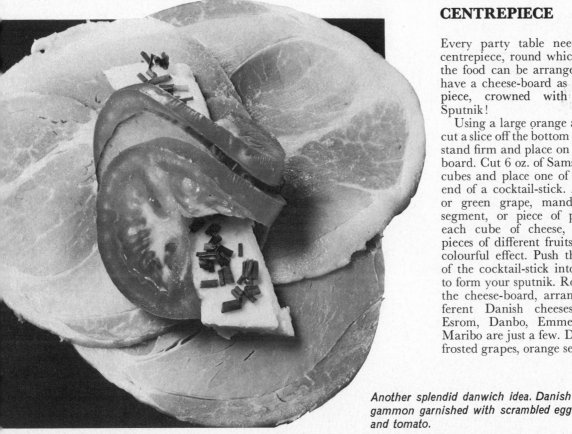

Another splendid danwich idea. Danish gammon garnished with scrambled egg and tomato.

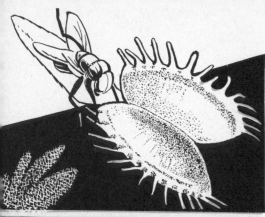

Venus's fly-traps are meat-eating plants found in America. The plants have leaves which are hinged together in two parts. When an insect lands on the leaves the hinges close, trapping the insect, which is then digested by the plant.

Courtplasters, or beauty-patches, were worn by fashionable ladies at the end of the seventeenth century. They were small patches of black silk which were stuck on the face with adhesive. They usually took the form of stars or hearts, but the larger ones were shaped as birds or cupids.

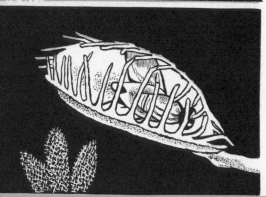

Perhaps one of the longest words is a word which describes a goulash, which is a Hungarian stew. The word is lopadotemachoselacho-galeokranioleipsanodrom-hypotrimmatosilphioparao-melitokatakechymenokichle-pikossyphophattoperistera-lektryonoptekephalliokigklo-peleiolagoiosiraiobaphetra-ganopterygon. The word has 182 letters and appears in a comedy by the Greek play-wright, Aristophanes.

To make one pound of honey a bee may have to travel 13,000 miles, or about four times the distance across Australia. Bees usually fly at a speed of about 12 miles per hour.

The smallest recorded height of a mature woman is 2 feet. The woman was Pauline Musters, who was born in 1876. When she died, in 1895, she weighed between $7\frac{1}{2}$ and 9 pounds.

FANCY THAT!

The Victoria is a water-lily which grows in rivers in South America. The floating leaves usually measure more than 6 feet across, and the plant bears pink and white flowers which usually measure more than 1 foot across.

In London markets, portering is the main mode of transportation of heavy weights. In Billingsgate fish market the porters carry large weights on their heads. They wear special hats and the baskets of fish are slotted, one on top of the other, into the hat. The pile of baskets may be many feet tall.

Chewing-gum is made from chicle, which is the juice of the sapota or sapodilla tree, which is found in parts of South America. Cuts are made in the tree bark and the sap is collected in containers at the base of the tree. The juice is boiled until it becomes very sticky and elastic in texture.

GRAB THAT GHOST

"I wonder who *has* bought the Old House," mused Marty Dean.

She was perched on the worn mounting-block in the cobbled stable-yard of St. Margaret's boarding school.

Kitty Brett, perched on the steps close by, tried to pull her plump, jolly face into a horrible grimace. "I think one of these mad scientists has moved in," she croaked. "Y'know— one of these nuts you see in the horror movies on television. He's probably got a pet monster."

Marty giggled. Kitty was good fun. Both girls were boarders at the school, and also keen Guides in the company attached to the school. They were waiting for one of their friends, Jenny Fustian. The trio had planned to walk into the village to buy ice-creams.

Marty jumped from the mounting-block as she spotted Jenny's long lanky figure coming from the direction of the school. "Hi! Come on, or we'll never get there and back before supper," shouted Marty.

Jenny broke into a run. She was a fine athlete, and her two friends encouraged her with a cheer as she covered the ground in a flying sprint.

"Phew, I'll *need* an ice-cream after all this exercise," said Jenny.

The three girls fell in step as they headed for the main gates of the school.

"We were discussing who might have bought the Old House," said Marty. "Any theories?"

Jenny shrugged. "Oh well, the whole school is buzzing with rumours, isn't it?" she remarked. "Take your pick, Marty—d'you fancy the

by Kay McGarry

idea that it's one of the Beatles seeking seclusion, or a retired spy, or a mad scientist?"

Marty pointed ahead to the thatched cottage that stood near the school gates. It had once been the lodge, in the days when St. Mary's had been a historic mansion. "I wonder if Miss Snafell can solve the mystery?" she said.

As they drew near, they could see the erect figure of their friend working in the garden. Before her retirement, Miss Amelia Snafell had been games mistress at St. Margaret's School. She greeted them with a cheerful wave of her garden-fork. "Any bruises from Friday?" she asked.

The girls laughed. On Friday, Miss Snafell had been at their Guide meeting to teach them some judo holds.

"No bruises," chuckled Marty. "But I'm still a bit airsick when I remember how high you threw me with that shoulder toss."

"You can call that the Snafell Special," said their friend. "Very useful in a tight corner."

"I say, Miss Snafell, have you heard who's bought the Old House?" asked Kitty.

The other's keen blue eyes twinkled. "As a matter of fact, I have," she admitted.

They pressed against the fence, eager for her news.

But Miss Snafell walked towards her trim front porch, saying: "Wait just a minute."

She came back with a parcel. "There's a new postman on this round, and he left this here by mistake while I was out shopping. It's for the Old House. Would you like to

drop it in there on your way past?"

"Oh, yes." Kitty reached for the parcel over the fence. They all craned their heads to read the address. It read: 'Dr. Dixon, The Old House, Cullacoombe'.

"What kind of doctor is he?" wondered Jenny.

"A scientist of some kind—or so I've heard," said Miss Snafell. "He's apparently retired now, and has been doing well as an inventor."

A few minutes later the three girls were swinging down the road towards Cullacoombe. "I wonder what he invents," mused Marty. "Wonder if we'll hear any weird clunks and bangs and blips while we're in class?"

"Why not?" nodded Kitty. "After all, the Old House is quite close to the school—as the crow flies."

"Miss Hendry was saying in history lesson that both buildings date back

to the Civil War," remarked Marty.

They had reached the crossroads, near the village duckpond, and were about to turn right towards the Old House, when a clod of earth hit Jenny on the shoulder. She jumped back, angrily brushing soil from her anorak and glaring round. A hoot of harsh laughter came from behind a bush and two long-haired youths appeared. They had other lumps of earth in their hands, and were obviously ready to throw them.

"What's the idea?" stormed Jenny.

"Target practice!" jeered one of the boys, who wore a shiny-peaked blue cap.

"The fair is coming to Culla-coombe, and we want to win all the coconuts, see?" sniggered the second youth. He hurled another clod at Marty, but she ducked.

"You stop that!" she flared.

"Yes, stop acting like babies!" snapped Kitty.

The second boy flushed. He doubled his bony fists, and advanced towards Kitty.

"Buzz off back to your precious boarding school, cissy!" he grated.

Kitty stood her ground calmly. Then, as the boy reached out to grab her, she neatly caught him by the wrist, pulled him off balance and sent him sprawling with a judo throw. He lay gasping.

His friend came into the attack more cautiously.

"Watch him!" urged Jenny, backing away.

Marty backed off too, for the youth was unbuckling his belt. He began to whirl it at Jenny, and Marty saw her chance.

She dashed at the attacker, crouching low to get the full effect of the 'Snafell Special'. It worked beautifully. The boy spun sideways from the shoulder toss. He hit the ground and went rolling towards the duck pond.

Splash! The green slime that covered the surface was sprayed onto the road as the bully flopped in. He sat up, gasping. His friend staggered over to help him out.

"Nice work!" chuckled Jenny. "But I think discretion is the better part of valour. We'd better go!"

As they walked away, the girls heard Peaked Cap yell: "I'll get even with you!"

The trio tried to laugh off the threat. But they felt a bit unnerved by the incident. "Phew. Thank goodness Miss Snafell taught us that bit of judo," said Kitty.

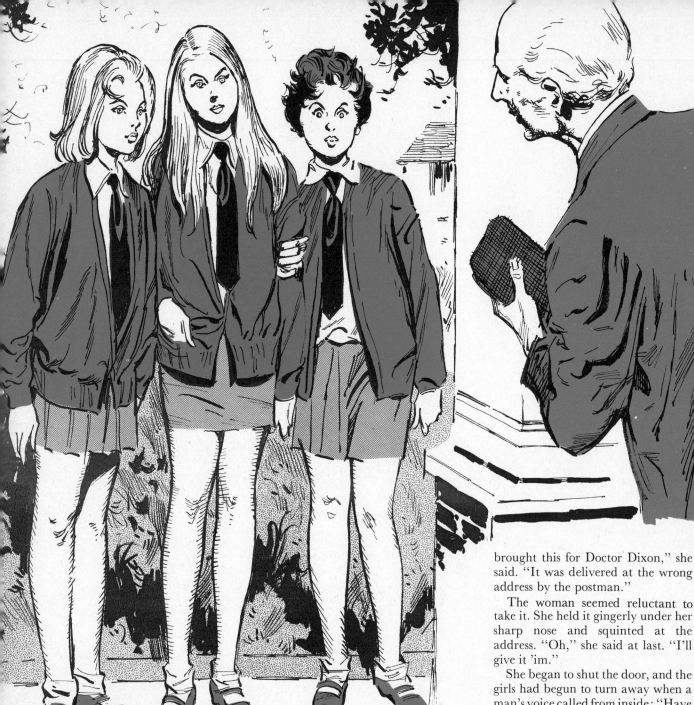

"It took the stuffing out of those two cowards, anyway," agreed Marty.

They forgot the attack as they turned in at the gates of the Old House. There was an air of mystery and seclusion about the place. The mullioned windows seemed to squint at the girls suspiciously from the black-and-white walls beneath the heavy-slated roof.

"Bit spooky, huh?" murmured Jenny, as she stepped into the porch and pulled at the bell-rope.

After a few moments the door was opened by a thin-faced woman in a flowered apron. She had obviously been in the middle of something, for she was wiping her rather red hands on the hem of her apron.

She looked at the three girls with a harassed frown. "Yes. What is it?" she asked.

Jenny held out the parcel. "We've brought this for Doctor Dixon," she said. "It was delivered at the wrong address by the postman."

The woman seemed reluctant to take it. She held it gingerly under her sharp nose and squinted at the address. "Oh," she said at last. "I'll give it 'im."

She began to shut the door, and the girls had begun to turn away when a man's voice called from inside: "Have we got visitors, Mrs. Bass?"

"Oh . . . it's only some girls with a parcel that went to the wrong address," they heard her explain.

The door opened, and their new neighbour appeared with the parcel in his hands. All three had to admit later that he was quite unlike what they had expected. There was nothing vague, or absent-minded, or untidy about Dr. Dixon. He was neat as a new pin—a slim, elegant man with an almost bald head fringed by a very becoming tonsure of curly grey hair.

"Very nice of you to have brought my parcel over," he said. "Won't you step in and have a drink of coke?"

They warmed to him immediately. Mrs. Bass had vanished—probably back to her housework. The inventor led the girls through a charming hall, and into a panelled room at the rear of the house. Furniture was lined against one wall, and packing cases half-full of books stood in the middle of a half-rolled carpet.

Dr. Dixon waved the girls to a settee and began to get bottles and glasses from a sideboard. "Hope you'll pardon the mess," he said cheerily. "I'm still unpacking."

"It must be a big job," offered Kitty.

"It is, my dear." The inventor smiled and uncapped the bottle with an expert turn of the wrist. He poured out the sparkling drink, and handed them their glasses.

"Are you *really* an inventor?" burst out Marty, unable to restrain her curiosity.

He flashed her a charming smile. "I like to think so," he nodded. "When you've finished that, I'll show you my workshop—my Ideas Factory, I call it."

"Oh yes, please," exclaimed Marty.

He poured himself a drink and sat on the end of an oak table. "And you girls are from St. Margaret's School?" he enquired.

They told him they were boarders there. Dr. Dixon listened with interest, and plied them with questions about the school building. "You see, I'm quite an enthusiast for old Tudor and Stuart houses," he explained. Then with a twinkle he added: "One reason why I moved into the Old House was the legend about a ghostly figure that walks the corridors."

The girls stopped sipping their drinks, and stared. "Honestly?" said Jenny. "A *real* ghost?"

"Well, so they say," said Dr. Dixon. "I'm hoping I get to see it. I'd rather like it to be some restless Cavalier, still searching for his King!"

Marty went back to her drink. Then she said: "Oh, they're just stories. We've got one at St. Mar-garet's. A ghost legend, I mean. Our history teacher Miss Hendry says the place was besieged by Cromwell during the Civil War, and the squire died."

"Yes, and the story is that his spirit still haunts the school," added Jenny.

"But nobody has ever seen it," put in Kitty.

Dr. Dixon finished his drink and stood up. "Ready to see my workshop?" he asked.

He led the way through more panelled rooms, and out of some french windows. They fell in step beside him as he led the way across the lawn towards a new-looking wooden hut.

They followed him inside, and saw long workbenches on each side of the hut. There was an astonishing selection of tools and materials, but everything was piled or ranged or hung in the same tidy manner that was revealed in the inventor's appearance.

He picked up a model of a life-raft from the bench. "This is my latest brain-storm!" he quipped. "A new kind of life-raft. That's what this paint is for . . . Here, watch!"

He dipped a brush into the can of paint before him, and brushed some onto the model. Then he held it in a dark corner of the hut. "Ooh, it glows!" exclaimed Kitty.

"Is it luminous paint?" asked Marty.

"Yes—but a special kind. I mixed it myself," said Dr. Dixon.

For the next ten minutes they listened eagerly as he explained some of his inventions. At last he said he would walk with them to the gates of the house.

"I hope you'll come back and see me," he said as they went. "I'd like to come to the school, too, and hunt for your ghost!"

They laughed. Kitty assured him they'd love to pay another visit.

He nodded, satisfied. "We'll be a bit more organised next time you

come," he promised. "My house-keeper—that's Mrs. Bass—has only just come to work for me, so there's quite a lot to do."

After they'd said goodbye and left, the girls were too full of the news of their visit to bother about ice-creams in the village.

"Let's get back and tell the rest of the school," urged Marty.

"They'll be green with envy," chuckled Jenny.

"Besides, we might tangle with those boys again in the village," remembered Kitty.

The rest of that evening passed quickly. When it became known that the trio had actually *met* the new occupant of the Old House, *and* seen his inventions, they became the centre of interest for the whole school. In fact, they were kept so busy talking about Dr. Dixon that there was no time to mention their other adventure with the bully boys.

Even in the dormitory, after lights-out, the excited whisperings went on.

"Oh, *do* give it a rest, and let us get some sleep," said Jenny with a yawn, punching her pillow to make it more comfortable.

"Besides, you'll probably meet the inventor yourselves," said Marty. "He said he wanted to visit the school. He's interested in our ghost."

That brought a chorus of groans. It was plain that nobody at St. Margaret's believed in the ghost.

At last silence fell on the dormitory. Jenny began to snore. Marty could hear her, for she lay in the bed opposite and couldn't get to sleep herself.

She was just dozing off, when a strange noise jerked her back to wakefulness. . .

She sat up, realising that the door was creaking open in the dark. "Who's that?" she whispered.

A low groan reached her ears. And the next moment she knew a chill of fear as a ghostly figure came gliding into view.

Marty could find no words to voice her terror and alarm. Her vocal chords seemed to have been frozen.

Meanwhile the apparition moved soundlessly towards the centre of the dormitory. It was all white, and glowed with an eerie light in the blackness of the room.

Suddenly a girl screamed.

Thankfully, Marty felt power return to her limbs—and her voice. "It's the ghost!" she gasped.

The shining figure was moving back towards the door. By this time the whole dormitory was waking up, as girls began to sob and shout.

As the ghost vanished, Marty slipped out of bed and reached for her dressing-gown.

Hands UP

Do your hands stand up to close inspection? Do they look well groomed and neat? If you give yourself a regular weekly or fortnightly manicure you will soon have hands and nails to be proud of.

Before beginning your manicure it is best to assemble all your equipment. You will need: cotton wool, polish-remover, emery-boards, cuticle-remover, orange-sticks, handcream, base coat, nail-enamel and top coat.

Step one. Moisten cotton wool with a good remover and remove old nail

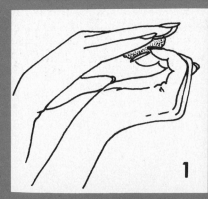

polish with firm strokes along the nail. Ensure that the nails are quite clean and free from old polish and wipe with a clean piece of cotton wool.

Step two. Using an emery-board, *not* a steel file, file lightly from side of nail to centre *only*. Never saw at nails, as this causes damage to the nails. Shape nails into a gently rounded shape. Wash hands in soapy water and dry well.

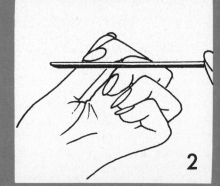

Step three. Using an orange-stick end wrapped in cotton wool, apply cuticle-remover to each nail. *Gently* push back cuticle with the other end of the orange-stick and dry nails gently with cotton wool.

Step four. Apply handcream liberally, not forgetting elbows, especially if they are rough. Smooth into the skin, remembering to remove any remaining grease from nails with cotton wool.

She felt a hand grab her arm, and Kitty's voice hissed in her ear: "Are you game to follow it?"

"Yes," said Marty.

Together they moved towards the dormitory door. Marty reached out and snapped on the lights. A gasp of relief came from the girls.

On the landing, Kitty stared round in open disbelief. "It can't have vanished," she said. "It only just went out of the door."

Marty stared at the panelled walls. "I suppose that's the trademark of a real ghost—being able to vanish into thin air," she remarked.

By this time the commotion from the dormitory had roused the teachers, and soon the landing was crowded with people—all talking loudly and excitedly, as they stared around.

It was arranged that two of the teachers should sleep in the dormitory that night.

But the ghost did not reappear.

The teachers found it impossible in the classrooms next day. All that the girls wanted to do was discuss the ghost. Miss Hendry did not even attempt to try a history lesson. She

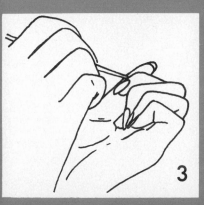

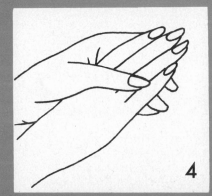

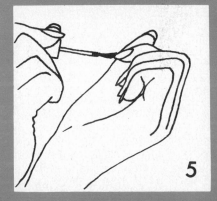

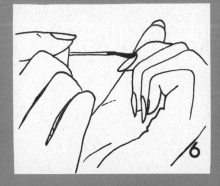

Step five. Apply base or under coat carefully and allow to dry thoroughly. Never apply nail polish directly on to the nails as this can make the nails dry and brittle.

Step six. Apply nail polish in long firm strokes from base of nail to tip, taking care to see that the polish is not streaky. Allow this coat to dry properly, then add a second coat if you wish. A top coat may now be added—this will prevent chipping.

Lastly, there is one golden rule for good hands and nails. Soap and water are the two things which do most damage to hands and nails, so it is important to apply handcream every time your hands have been in water. This puts back the moisture which soap and water take away. If you follow these rules your hands and nails will soon look perfectly groomed and beautiful.

found herself trying to throw cold water on the idea she had once put forward in class that the ghost legend of St. Margaret's stemmed from the death of the squire during the Civil War siege.

"Really, girls, you *know* there are no such things as ghosts," she said for the fiftieth time.

Just then the bell went for end of lessons.

Outside the classroom, Marty beckoned to Kitty and Jenny. "Come with me—I've got an idea," she said.

They followed her upstairs towards the dormitory. On the landing Marty stopped. She was staring hard at the panelled wall.

"What's the idea?" asked Jenny.

Marty went closer to the wall, searching keenly. "I noticed a clue last night, but I didn't want to say anything to the teachers until we'd had a chance to check it out," she said.

"You've been watching too many television thrillers," said Jenny.

Marty did not reply. She reached out, tugged something carefully from the panelling, and held it up. "Look —a thread. Cotton, I think. And it was caught between those two panels," she said.

"A white thread? Wonder how it got there?" asked Kitty. Then her eyes widened as the solution dawned. "Hey! A secret panel!" she exclaimed.

Marty and Jenny were already running their hands over the beading at the top of the panelling.

"Press hard!" Marty was urging her friend when she felt a section of the beading give under her own probing fingers. There was a click, and the panel slid aside.

"So that's where the ghost vanished," crowed Kitty.

"Marty, you're a born detective," praised Jenny.

"And all good detectives come prepared," quipped Marty, producing a torch from her pocket. "Come on. Let's see where this leads to."

She ducked into the narrow opening, to find a flight of stone steps leading down. It led to a low, brick-lined passage.

"Phew, it smells damp and horrid," choked Kitty. "You're not going along there, are you, Marty?"

But her friend was already moving ahead with the torch. "Can't turn back now," she said over her shoulder. "Come on. It's quite good."

Kitty hurried after the other two, and the strange journey continued in silence.

Suddenly Marty stopped. "Aha!" she exclaimed. "So *this* is what the ghost used."

The beam of her torch was resting on a white cotton sheet that hung from a nail in the wall. "That's where the thread in the panelling must have come from," exclaimed Jenny.

"Yes. And watch this," said Marty. She switched off her torch. The others gave a gasp as they saw the white sheet glowing in the sudden darkness.

"Luminous paint!" exclaimed Kitty.

Marty snapped on the torch. "Quite. And I'm willing to bet that this passage leads us out close to a good supply of that paint—the Doctor's workshop!" she said.

Only a few paces beyond the sheet they came to a dead end. The torch showed a wooden barrier. It was thick with old cobwebs, which showed signs of having been recently disturbed.

"Here goes," breathed Marty, pushing hard at the barrier. It slid aside with a grating sound, and daylight flooded into the passage.

The girls hurried out to find them-

Peter was completely unprepared for any attack, as were what few troops he had with him, and they were quite unequal to Catherine's army. Peter was forced to surrender and abdicate his throne.

Although a prisoner, Peter was allowed to live as befitted his rank, but one evening he forced a quarrel with a member of Catherine's household. A fight ensued and during the struggle Peter was killed. Catherine now had absolute power throughout all Russia, and she ruled ruthlessly, yet with a love for her people which gained her the affectionate nickname of 'Little Mother of all the Russias'.

Catherine set about trying to improve conditions for the peasants in Russia. She opened a hospital for destitute children, the first ever in Russia, where orphaned children were well cared for and taught a trade so that they might make an honest living.

During the early days of her marriage, Catherine had often told her few faithful friends that she believed the reason for her husband's spiteful behaviour sprang from his feeling of inferiority, because of his appearance. Peter's face had been badly scarred as a result of a bad attack of small-pox, and when Catherine heard of a new vaccine which prevented this dreaded disease, she herself was vaccinated so that others would follow her example.

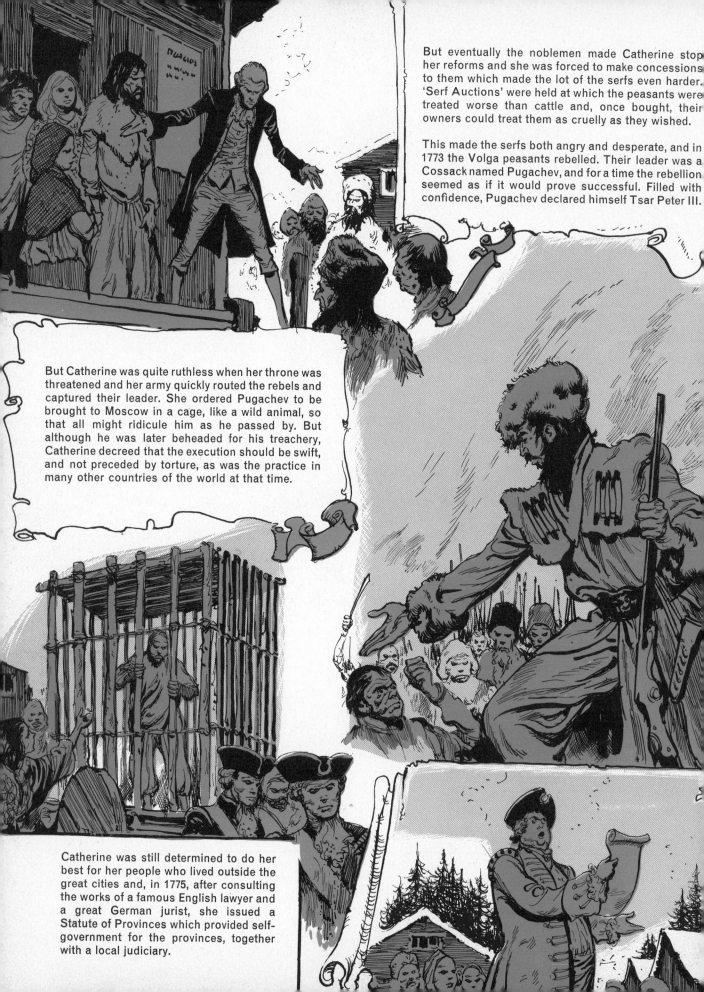

But eventually the noblemen made Catherine stop her reforms and she was forced to make concessions to them which made the lot of the serfs even harder. 'Serf Auctions' were held at which the peasants were treated worse than cattle and, once bought, their owners could treat them as cruelly as they wished.

This made the serfs both angry and desperate, and in 1773 the Volga peasants rebelled. Their leader was a Cossack named Pugachev, and for a time the rebellion seemed as if it would prove successful. Filled with confidence, Pugachev declared himself Tsar Peter III.

But Catherine was quite ruthless when her throne was threatened and her army quickly routed the rebels and captured their leader. She ordered Pugachev to be brought to Moscow in a cage, like a wild animal, so that all might ridicule him as he passed by. But although he was later beheaded for his treachery, Catherine decreed that the execution should be swift, and not preceded by torture, as was the practice in many other countries of the world at that time.

Catherine was still determined to do her best for her people who lived outside the great cities and, in 1775, after consulting the works of a famous English lawyer and a great German jurist, she issued a Statute of Provinces which provided self-government for the provinces, together with a local judiciary.

She also wanted to make Russia a strong foreign power, respected and feared by friends and foes alike. By treaties and by wars she acquired parts of Poland, protected the Christians from attack by the Turks and gained for Russia lands right up to the Black Sea.

Yet Catherine was also a woman of culture, corresponding with Voltaire and other famous men of letters. She founded St. Petersburg Public Library, and she herself wrote fables and histories. Today there are still letters of hers to be seen which show her quick wit and intelligence.

And beneath her seemingly ruthless exterior Catherine had a tender heart for anyone she held dear. Although never on good terms with her son Paul, she loved his two sons, Alexander and Constantine. She was always buying them presents and loved playing with them whenever her duties permitted.

Anything she did with her grandchildren was always reported by Catherine to other rulers, and when she found some clothes for the baby Alexander which were particularly suitable, she insisted on sending the pattern for the clothes to the King of Sweden and the Prince of Prussia!

No expense was ever spared to gratify Catherine's slightest wish, be it a new palace or the latest gown; yet in some ways the Empress was surprisingly humble. In order to get the most out of every day Catherine would rise at five o'clock each morning, but rather than awaken her sleeping servants she would light the fire herself . . . just like an ordinary Russian peasant woman.

On one such morning, as Catherine drew back the heavy curtains to let in the first light of the day, she saw a spring flower pushing its way through the lawn. "Such an effort deserves recognition," murmured Catherine to herself, and she immediately ordered a sentry to be posted on the lawn to guard the flower in case it was mistakenly plucked or trodden upon.

An amusing result of this incident was recorded some sixty years later when it was discovered that a sentry was still standing on the lawn . . . no one had ever thought to rescind Catherine's order.

In 1787, Catherine made a voyage down the Dnieper and a grand tour of southern Russia with the Austrian Emperor, Joseph II. Barren deserts became great cities just for the one day that Catherine passed through, and everywhere she was warmly welcomed. To show her appreciation of this display of affection from her people, Catherine told her coachmen to shower golden coins on to the cheering crowds.

She also laid the foundation-stone of a mighty city to be named Ekaterinaslaw in her honour. But the Austrian Emperor, who laid the second stone, prophesied that this stone would also be the last, for, as Joseph had shrewdly guessed, there was never enough money to complete the city.

But times were changing, bringing with them events such as the French Revolution which, despite Catherine's liberal ideals, filled her with horror and disgust, and which resulted in her imprisoning writers such as Radischev, who at one time she would have praised highly for his liberal views.

It seemed that the wheel had come full circle, for now it was Catherine's turn, as Empress, to find a suitable bridegroom for her young grand-daughter, Alexandrina. As she waited with Alexandrina in the Winter Palace to sign the marriage contract with the envoys sent by King Gustav Adolphus of Sweden, Catherine must surely have thought of the day, over thirty years before, when she had arrived for the first time at the court of the Empress Elizabeth.

However, the demands made in the contract by Catherine proved too great for the Swedish king and he refused to sign. Catherine fell into such a rage on hearing this that she fell seriously ill.

When she died a few weeks later, in the wintry month of November 1796, thousands mourned their 'Little Mother of all the Russias'. She had done much to strengthen the position of Russia throughout the world, and for her efforts as a reformer, a legislator, a woman of culture with a great love of the arts, and a brilliant and shrewd conqueror, she can truly be called Catherine the Great.

SCENE-STEALING SUEDE

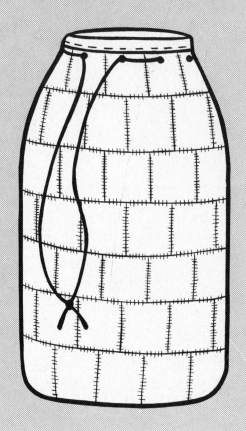

BRENDA UTTLEY GIVES STEP-BY-STEP IN-STRUCTIONS FOR MAKING AN ATTRACTIVE AND USEFUL BAG.

By using up seemingly worthless scraps you can make a bag which will make you the envy of all your friends. Not only that; you can make your bag for a fraction of the cost of a similar bag in the shops. You will need some suede scraps—which are usually available from handicraft shops, and which cost next to nothing—and a piece of leather thonging. The only other thing you'll need is, of course, patience!

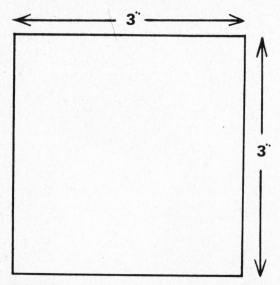

FIGURE 1

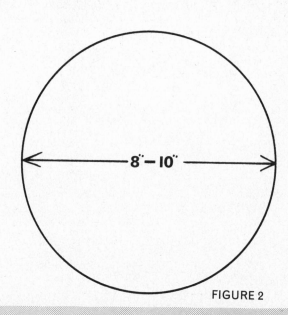

FIGURE 2

Begin by taking your suede scraps and cutting from them squares which should measure 3 or 4 inches along each side. The actual size of your squares is really up to you, but remember that whatever size you choose, all your squares must be the same size (figure 1).

Next you must cut out a circular piece of suede, which will form the base of your bag. This should be about 8 or 10 inches in diameter, but again the size is really up to you. If you haven't any compasses a dinner-plate may be useful to measure out your circle (figure 2).

Now, remembering to keep the two suede sides of the material together, begin to sew your suede squares into strips. Use small neat stitches (figure 3) because if your stitches are large and untidy your bag will not be strong and may soon rip.

FIGURE 3

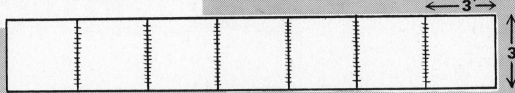

FIGURE 4

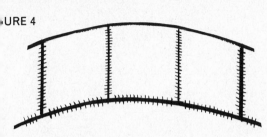

Now keep adding on other strips of squares until your bag is as deep as you want it, usually about 10 or 12 inches (figure 5).

FIGURE 5

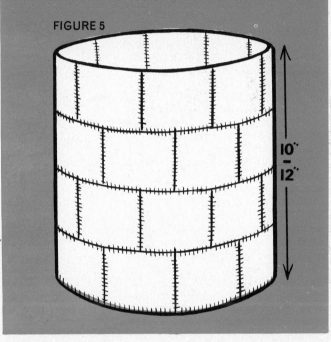

Next join your first completed strip to the base, again remembering to keep the two suede sides of the material together while you sew them. You should now be able to see your bag taking shape (figure 4).

When your bag is as deep as you want it, cut long strips of suede about 1 inch wide. Fold these in half lengthways and over the top edge of your bag. Sew these along the top edge of your bag, so that you are sewing through three thicknesses (figure 6). This forms a strong binding which means that you will not have any raw edges, which would look very untidy.

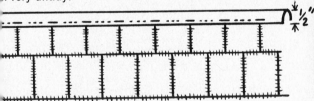

FIGURE 6

With a hot skewer make a series of small holes about 3 inches apart, just below the binding (figure 7).

Next take a long leather thong and thread it in and out of the holes. Knot the two ends of the thong so that it forms a drawstring (figure 8).

Finally, you may stiffen the base of your bag with a piece of stiff cardboard cut to the same measurement as your base.

FIGURE 7

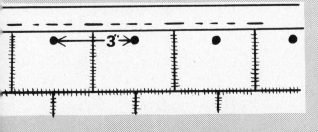

FIGURE 8

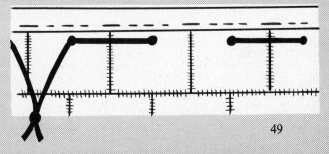

Pretty and Practical Patchwork

Have you ever thought what a pity it is to waste all the pieces of lovely material left over from dressmaking? Well, here's an idea—why not make them up into a patchwork apron for yourself? It's easy to do, and it's good fun too!

The first thing is to make a hexagonal shape (six-sided) in cardboard, and then, using this as a pattern, make lots of the shapes in paper.

Choose your pieces of material, and be careful not to mix pieces that will wash with pieces that won't! If you have a pair of pinking shears at home use them to cut your material—if not choose fabrics that don't fray easily.

Cut out the material round your paper shapes, allowing $\frac{1}{4}$ inch for turnings all the way round (figure 1).

The next step is to sew the material on to the paper as in figure 2. Use big tacking stitches and don't spend a lot of time making them very neat, because you'll be taking them out when you've finished your sewing.

When you have as many pieces as you think you'll need you can start to arrange them, and you'll see your work beginning to take shape. Put all the pieces on a table, and move them around till you find the best arrangement. You may like to have a section of one type of material in the centre—like figure 3. Or you may invent a design of your own. It's important to sort your pieces out before you sew them up—or you may end up with just a jumble of different colours and designs!

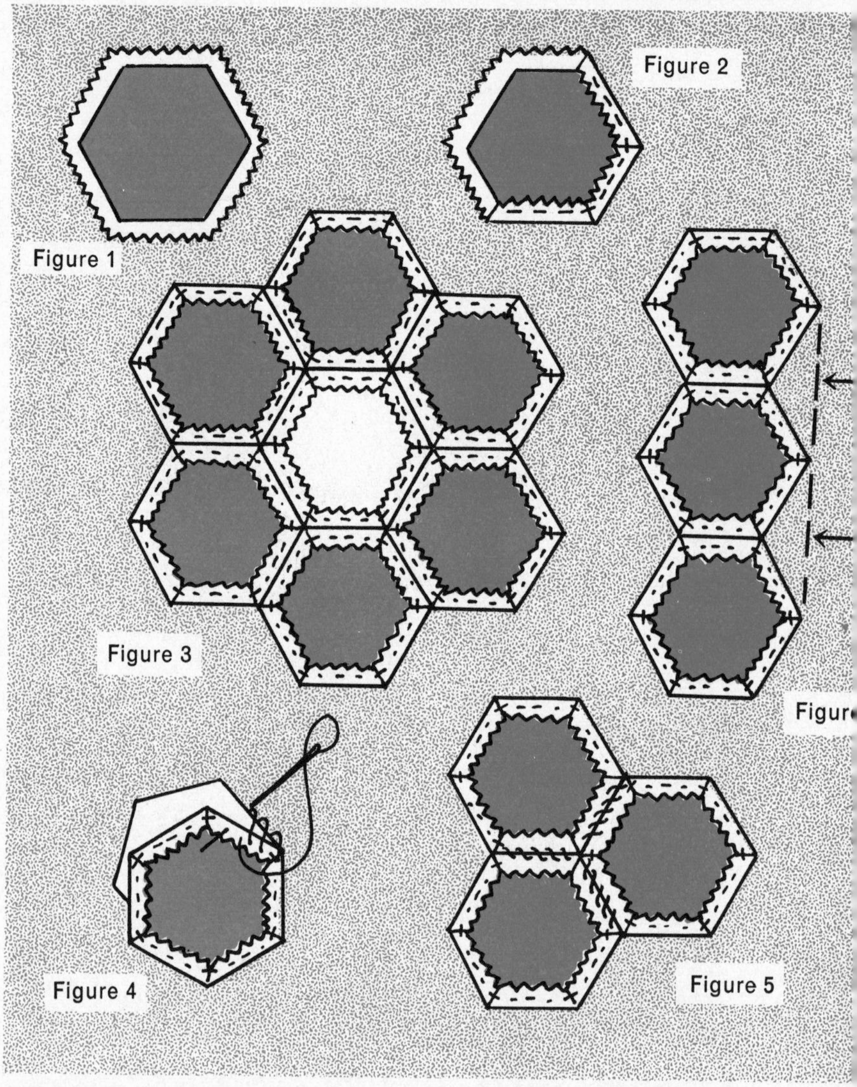

Join the pieces together, using a fine needle and light coloured thread. Be careful to use small, neat stitches so that they won't be seen on the right side of the work (figure 4). And make sure that your stitches are close together, so that the seams will be quite firm. Go on like this (figure 5) until your piece of patchwork is complete.

Now to make a really professional job of it you can line the patchwork with a piece of material. This will make it stronger, and it will last longer.

If you haven't got a large enough piece—and it will have to be about $\frac{1}{2}$ inch bigger all round than the patchwork—you may be able to buy a cheap remnant at the store in your town. Or you can join strips of material together to make one piece. Hem all round the

Figure 1

Figure 2

Figure 3

Figure 4

Figure 5

edges of the lining piece so that it looks neat and tidy.

Tack all the odd end pieces of the patchwork underneath so that the sides are quite straight. Or you could make smaller pieces to fit in the odd spaces if you want the piece to be a little bigger (figure 6).

Then you put the two wrong sides (lining and patchwork) together, and join them all round three sides with small, neat stitches. Now your work will look like a very gay pillow-case! Turn it inside out on to the right sides, and overstitch the last side. Do this

very carefully, because these stitches will show more than the others. Take out all your tacking stitches, sew on two long strips of ribbon, or hemmed material, and your pretty and practical apron is ready to wear!

If you enjoyed doing patchwork there are lots more things you can use it for—you could make a coverlet for a little girl's doll's pram or, if you're very ambitious, for your own bed! And of course you can make different designs and use all sorts of different shapes and sizes to make your patchwork different every time!

50

La Belle Dame Sans Merci

by John Keats

John Keats was born in London on 31st October 1795. His father, a livery-stable keeper, died when John was quite young. His mother re-married, but soon separated from her second husband, and John, together with his four younger brothers and sisters, went to live with his grandmother. John was unsettled by this instability in his life and was prone to periods of depression. He later remarked on the "horrid morbidity" which he had recognised in himself, even at this early stage in his life.

John attended Clarke's School in Enfield, where he formed a lasting friendship with Charles Cowden Clarke, the headmaster's son. In his early school career John spent most of his time fighting with his class-mates, but his work improved tremendously when he was reunited with his mother. His joy at having his mother back with the family again was, however, short-lived, for she fell ill with tuberculosis. She died in 1810, when John was fifteen. Once again Keats' new-found happiness was lost.

In the summer, Keats left school and became apprenticed to Thomas Hammond, the family surgeon. During his apprenticeship Keats was introduced to poetry. His old friend Clarke took him to a reading of Edmund Spenser's poetry; its effect on Keats was great. He began to experiment with different poetic forms—in fact his desire to become a poet was so great that he once told his brothers that if he did not become a poet he would kill himself. In 1815 he completed his apprenticeship and took a position at Guy's Hospital.

Poetry, however, began to occupy an increasing amount of his time and eventually, after having one or two of his earlier poems published, he made an important decision. He decided to give up what promised to be a distinguished career as a surgeon so that he could devote all his time to poetry. This decision meant that he was left with very little money but, supported by his family and friends, he published, at the age of twenty-two, his first volume of poems. Unfortunately it aroused no interest whatever. This period of his life was one of great intellectual activity, but soon family troubles again became apparent.

His brother George married and emigrated to America, and John returned from a holiday in Scotland in 1818 to find his other brother, Tom, dying of tuberculosis. Tom died in December of the same year and Keats went to live with his friend Charles Brown. Keats again went through a period of extreme restlessness and depression, during which he formulated some of his deepest and most profound comments on life. It was during this period in his life that Keats wrote *La Belle Dame sans Merci*.

Keats met and fell in love with Fanny Brawne, his next-door neighbour. Their love had a great calming effect on Keats, restoring some of the happiness which was missing from his life. Once more, however, his new-found happiness was marred by material problems. His brother George was speculating unwisely in America and money was short. In an attempt to make some money, Keats collaborated with Charles Brown in the writing of a play, *Otho the Great*. This activity spurred Keats to revise all his poetry, and to write many new poems.

He was, however, heading for disaster. While nursing his brother Tom, he had contracted tuberculosis, and he fell ill while holidaying in the Isle of Wight. His illness and his love for Fanny, who had stayed in London, brought back the morbidity of tempera-

ment to which he was prone. He returned to London to be nursed by Fanny and her mother, but showed little or no improvement. It was decided that he should spend the winter in Italy.

By now his poetry had begun to attract favourable reviews; but Keats was too ill to care. He was nursed in Rome by a young painter friend, Joseph Severn, and although he rallied slightly in the better weather there was no real improvement in his condition. He eventually died in Severn's arms, on 23rd February 1821. He was buried in the English Protestant Cemetery in Rome. The epitaph which he had written himself was engraved on his tombstone—"Here lies one whose name was writ in water".

His writing life had lasted for a year or so before England was robbed too early of one of her best-loved poets. True appreciation of Keats' poetry was to come after his tragic death, but he was always confident that it would come. He once remarked to a friend, with perhaps more foresight than he at that time thought, "I think I shall be among the English poets at my death," which he indeed was, and still is.

Keats' Poetry

John Keats is widely acknowledged as one of the most remarkable of the English Romantic poets. His poems show him to be a poet of powerful and deep feeling. He tended, through his poetry, to transfer unaltered impressions of what he felt and saw to the reader, with no apparent intervention from him. The effect of this is that his poetry conveys to the reader a mood, feeling or vision exactly as Keats saw or felt it.

A poet who had known great happi-

ness throughout his life would probably tend to write cheerful poems, because happiness was the feeling he knew best. In the same way Keats' life was for the most part unhappy and sorrowful, and so most of his poems tend to be thought of by some people as sentimental and melancholic.

Nevertheless one cannot say that Keats' poems are boring. They create great atmosphere, and one is always aware of his appreciation of beautiful things, be they spiritual or material.

La Belle Dame sans Merci

This poem, written on 21st April 1818, was one of the most spontaneous and unconscious of all Keats' poems. He drew his inspiration from many sources, but it is almost certain that on this occasion he drew his inspiration from his reading of Dante's *Inferno*, which impressed him greatly. The poem was written late at night when Keats was very tired, and was contained in a letter to his brother George.

The poem takes the form of a lyric—a short poem of a musical and rhythmic nature which expresses the poet's own feelings exactly. The poem has a fairly steady rhythm, broken only by the striking and beautiful last lines of each verse or stanza. This irregular four-syllable line in the rhyme-scheme gives the poem its particular character.

Where poetry is concerned, it is doubtful if any two people would ever agree absolutely on the exact meaning of any one poem. Different people may see different things in the same poem —poetry is essentially what the poet conveys to each individual. For this reason, interpretations of this poem may vary greatly. When you have read through it you will have formed your own ideas on what Keats meant to convey.

Who do you think the lady really was? Do you think that the knight-at-arms ever actually met the lady, or was he dreaming all the time? No one is able to answer these questions with certainty; we all have to form our own opinions. The only thing which is certain is that John Keats achieved what he set out to do—to give pleasure to his readers in many lands and over many years.

La Belle Dame Sans Merci

O what can ail thee, knight-at-arms,
Alone and palely loitering?
The sedge has wither'd from the lake,
And no birds sing.

O what can ail thee, knight-at-arms!
So haggard and so woebegone?
The squirrel's granary is full,
And the harvest's done.

I see a lily on thy brow
With anguish moist and fever-dew,
And on thy cheeks a fading rose
Fast withereth too.

I met a lady in the meads,
Full beautiful—a faery's child,
Her hair was long, her foot was light,
And her eyes were wild.

I made a garland for her head,
And bracelets too, and fragrant zone;
She look'd at me as she did love,
And made sweet moan.

I set her on my pacing steed,
And nothing else saw all day long,
For sidelong would she bend, and sing
A faery's song.

She found me roots of relish sweet,
And honey wild, and manna dew,
And sure in language strange she said—
"I love thee true."

She took me to her elfin grot,
And there she wept, and sigh'd full sore,
And there I shut her wild wild eyes
With kisses four.

And there she lullèd me asleep,
And there I dream'd—Ah! woe betide!
The latest dream I ever dream'd
On the cold hill's side.

I saw pale kings and princes too,
Pale warriors, death-pale were they all;
They cried—"La Belle Dame sans Merci
Hath thee in thrall!"

I saw their starved lips in the gloam,
With horrid warning gapèd wide,
And I awoke and found me here,
On the cold hill's side.

And this is why I sojourn here,
Alone and palely loitering,
Though the sedge has wither'd from the lake,
And no birds sing.

John Keats

53

Hook that Suit

Crochet is certainly the scene for the swinging seventies, so why not step out in style with this scene-stealing trendsetter. If you can knit, then I'm sure you'll find crochet easy to master, and if you can't knit, well I still think crochet is easier once you get the hang of it, and perhaps mum will be able to give you a helping hand. And if you can already crochet . . . well, what are you waiting for!

Original Shade Nos. Sirdar 032 Ivory and 115 Delphi Blue

BLAZER

To fit

Bust	30	32	34	ins.
Length	20	22	24	ins.
Sleeve	14	15	16	ins.

MATERIALS

Double Crepe *Wool*

shade A	19	20	22	balls
shade B	1	1	1	ball

1 No. 9 (3·50) Crochet Hook.
6 Buttons.

TROUSERS
To fit

Hips	31	33	35	ins.
Inner Leg seam	22	23½	25	ins.
Outer Leg measurement				
	32	34	36	ins.

MATERIALS

Double Crepe *Wool* 19 20 21 balls
1 No. 9 (3·50) and No. 10 (3·00) Crochet Hook.
8 Buttons.
Waist length of elastic ¾ inch wide.
THE TENSION FOR THIS DESIGN IS 5 sts to 1 inch.
Check your tension—if less stitches use a finer hook, if more stitches use a coarser hook.

ABBREVIATIONS

ch chain	**dc** double crochet
½-tr half treble	**ss** slip stitch or
rep repeat	single crochet
beg beginning	**st(s)** stitch(es)
dec decrease	

inc increase by working twice into 1 stitch
N.B. For the smallest size read the instructions as given.
For the larger sizes read the figures within the brackets.

BLAZER
THE BACK
Make 84 (89, 94) ch with A yarn.
1st Row (right side). Work 1 ½-tr into 3rd ch from hook, then 1 ½-tr into every ch to end. 83 (88, 93) ½-tr. Turn.
Proceed in rows of ½-tr, beg each row with 2 ch to stand for 1st ½-tr, and working last ½-tr into 2nd of turning ch. Continue until work measures 13 (14½, 16) inches, finishing after a wrong side row.

Shape Armholes
Ss to 6th st, 2 ch, work until 5 sts remain. Turn. Dec once at both ends of next 5 (6, 7) rows. 63 (66, 69) sts. Work 20 (21, 22) rows without shaping.

Shape Shoulders
Ss to 7th st, 2 ch, work until 6 sts remain. Turn.
Rep this row once, 39 (42, 45) sts now remain, central 27 (28, 29) being for neck, and 6 (7, 8) each side for shoulders. Fasten off.

THE POCKET LINING
(Work 2 alike)
Make 23 ch with A yarn. Work 4½ inches in rows of 22 ½-tr, finishing after a wrong side row. Fasten off.

THE LEFT FRONT
Make 56 (59, 62) ch with A yarn. Work 4½ inches in rows of 55 (58, 61) ½-tr, finishing after a wrong side row.

Join Pocket
Work 4 (6, 8) ½-tr, miss next 22 sts and work across sts of pocket in place of them, work remaining 29 (30, 31) sts. Proceed until work is 4 rows shorter than Back to armholes.

Shape Neck
Work 4 rows, decreasing once at front edge on 1st and 3rd rows.

Shape Armhole
Ss to 6th st, 2 ch, work to end, decreasing once at front edge. Dec at both ends of next 5 (6, 7) rows. 37 (38, 39) sts. Working side edge straight, dec once at front edge on every row until 18 (19, 20) sts remain. Work 1 (2, 3) rows without shaping.

Shape Shoulder
1st Row Ss to 7th st, 2 ch, work to end. Turn.
2nd Row Work 6 (7, 8) sts. Fasten off.

THE RIGHT FRONT
Work as Left Front reversing shapings and position of pocket and making 3 evenly-spaced buttonholes, 1st 1½ inches from lower edge, last 1 inch below beg of front shaping. Buttonholes are worked thus: 2 ch, 2 ½-tr, 3 ch, miss 3 sts, work to end. In next row work 3 ½-tr over buttonhole.

THE SLEEVES (Both alike)
Make 42 (45, 46) ch with A yarn. Work 6 rows of 41 (44, 45) ½-tr. Inc once at both ends of next and every 6th (5th, 5th) row following until there are 57 (62, 67) sts. Proceed until 13½ (14½, 15½) inches.

Shape Top
Ss to 6th st, 2 ch, work until 5 sts remain. Turn. Dec once at both ends of next 17 (19, 21) rows. 13 (14, 15) sts. Fasten off.

TO COMPLETE
Work 2 rows dc in B yarn along pocket tops and round lower edges of sleeves.

Press work with a hot iron under a damp cloth.

Join side, shoulder and sleeve seams. Set sleeves into armholes. Sew pocket linings in position.

With right side of work facing, with A yarn work 60 (68, 76) dc along right front edge as far as beg of shaping, 48 (53, 58) along shaped edge of right front, 27 (28, 29) across back of neck, 48 (53, 58) along shaped edge of left front, and 60 (68, 76) along remainder of left front. Fasten off.

Work 2 rows dc in B yarn along lower edge.

Work 2 rows dc in B yarn all round fronts and back neck edge.

Press seams. Sew on buttons.

THE TROUSERS

THE RIGHT LEG

Make 65 (68, 71) ch with No. 9 hook.

1st Row (right side). Work 1 ½-tr into 3rd ch from hook, then 1 ½-tr into every ch to end. 64 (67, 70) sts. Turn.

Proceed in rows of ½-tr, beg each row with 2 ch to stand for 1st ½-tr, and working last ½-tr in 2nd of turning ch. Work 1 inch. Inc once at both ends of next and every 4th row following until there are 100 (105, 110) sts. Proceed until work measures 22 (23½, 25) inches along side edges, or required length for inner leg seam, finishing after a wrong side row.

Next Row Ss to 5th st, 2 ch, work until 4 sts remain. Turn. Work 1 row. Dec at both ends of next and every alternate row until 82 (87, 92) sts remain, finishing after a wrong side row.**

Divide for Opening

Work 37 (40, 43) sts, turn. Proceed on these sts for Front. Work 1 more row. Dec once at both ends of next and every 4th row following until 31 (34, 37) sts remain. Now work front edge straight. Continue to dec at side edge on every 4th row until 29 (32, 35) sts remain. Continue until 9 (9½, 10) inches from beg of decreasing, measured on the straight, finishing after a wrong side row. Fasten off.

Join yarn to inner edge of remaining 45 (47, 49) sts for Back. Work 2 rows. Dec at both ends of next and every 4th row following until 35 (37, 39) sts remain. Proceed until 9 (9½, 10) inches from first decreasing, finishing after a wrong side row.

Shape Back

1st Row Ss to 6th (8th, 10th) st, work to end. Turn.

2nd Row Work 24 sts, turn.

3rd Row Ss to 7th st, work to end. Turn.

4th Row Work 12 sts, turn.

5th Row Ss to 7th st, work remaining 6 sts. Fasten off.

THE LEFT LEG

Work as Right Leg as far as **.

Divide for Opening

Work 45 (47, 49) sts, turn. Proceed as Back of right leg until 35 (37, 39) sts remain and work measures 9 (9½, 10) inches from first decreasing, finishing after a wrong side row.

Shape Back

1st Row Work 30 sts, turn.

2nd Row Ss to 7th st, work to end. Turn.

3rd Row Work 18 sts, turn.

4th Row Ss to 7th st, work 6 sts. Fasten off.

Join yarn to inner edge of remaining 37 (40, 43) sts. Complete front to correspond with front of right leg, reversing shapings.

TO COMPLETE

Press work with a hot iron under a damp cloth. Join back, front and leg seams.

With No. 10 hook, beg with right side of work facing, work 6 rows dc along waist edge of back and front.

With No. 10 hook, beg with right side of work facing, work 2 rows of 36 (38, 40) dc along front edge of side opening on right leg. In next row make buttonholes thus: 2 ch, 1 dc into next dc, * 2 ch, miss 2 dc, 1 dc into each of next 7 dc. Rep from * twice more, 2 ch, miss 2 dc, 1 dc into each of 5 (7, 9) remaining dc. Turn. In next row work 2 dc into each buttonhole. Work 2 more rows dc. Fasten off.

Complete front of side opening on left leg in same way, but working buttonhole row thus: 2 ch, 1 dc into each of 1st 4 (6, 8) dc, * 2 ch, miss 2 dc, 1 dc into each of next 7 dc. Rep from * twice more, 2 ch, miss 2 dc, 1 dc into each of 2 remaining dc.

Work 1 row of 36 (38, 40) dc along back of each side opening.

Attach elastic to wrong side of back waistband with herringbone casing, and sew in position at each end. Attach elastic to front waistband in same way, sewing ends to inner edges of buttonholes. To avoid strain on the waistband beyond buttonholes it is advisable to back ends of waistband with an inch or so of ribbon, cutting buttonholes in ribbon.

Sew down base of plackets.

Press. Sew on buttons.

THE CASE OF THE DISAPPEARING CASHIERS

Mr. Palfrey, of Palfrey, Mason & Wood Ltd., studied the card presented by Zoe.

"So you're from the Allen Detective Agency?" he brought out slowly. "Doesn't your concern employ male detectives?"

"Oh, yes," Zoe fibbed. "We have at least a dozen in our employ, only they all happen to be engaged upon other cases at the moment. I was sent along to get the facts, that's all. One of our best private investigators will then be assigned to the case."

"Oh, I see . . ." murmured Mr. Palfrey, apparently satisfied with her explanation. "I'd like this little matter handled very discreetly. It concerns one of our employees—our Head Cashier, Mr. Loftman, in fact. He's been with us for over twenty years, and we'd like to be very sure of our facts before making any accusations."

"I understand," Zoe said gravely. "You can rely on us."

"Good! Now, first of all I'd like you to take a look at this."

He handed her a letter addressed to the firm. Zoe noticed that the postmark was Sydney, Australia, and the address was typewritten.

It may interest you to know that your Head Cashier is spending at least £50 per week on lottery tickets out here. Seeing that he only earns £15, this leaves £35 to be accounted for. Suggest you have someone check the books.

The note, which had been written by hand, block capitals having been used throughout, was signed 'A Friend'.

"I suppose you followed this person's advice and had someone check the books?" Zoe ventured, handing the letter back to him.

"Yes, we did . . ." Mr. Palfrey said

57

heavily. "I had Mr. French, our assistant cashier, run through them."

"And?" Zoe prompted him.

"We found a great number of discrepancies. It would appear that someone has been helping himself every week to the tune of about £40."

"Hmmm . . . looks rather bad for your Mr. Loftman, doesn't it?" remarked Zoe.

"Yes, I suppose it does . . ." he was compelled to admit. "But, before jumping to any conclusions, I'd like your agency to track down the writer of this note. I'm a little curious as to the whys and wherefores, if you know what I mean. He seems to know quite a lot about our affairs. I'm also intrigued why a stranger from the other side of the world should have our interests at heart."

"It is rather odd, now you come to mention it . . . Maybe he's an ex-employee of yours who migrated to Australia?"

"I doubt it. Most of our staff have been with us since they were boys. They're all conscientious workers, and we haven't had to sack one for years. However, I'll check up on the matter for you."

"Do you happen to know whether Mr. Loftman was ever instrumental in getting someone the sack?" Zoe persisted.

"I doubt it, but I'll look into the matter—"

"Good!" Zoe said, getting to her feet. "In the meantime we'll get in touch with the Australian C.I.B. Although I'm afraid we're present-ing them with a pretty hard nut. A solitary letter of that sort isn't much to go on. Which reminds me, you'd better let me have the letter."

Mr. Palfrey handed over the letter. "Well, do the best you can," he said, accompanying her to the door.

"We always do," she assured him pertly.

It was not until a fortnight later that she was able to convey news of a sort to Mr. Palfrey.

"The Australian C.I.B. have been most helpful," she informed him over the telephone. "They've checked with the lottery people; apparently they run a sweepstake every day in Sydney. They sell millions of tickets

every week, and it would be asking too much to expect them to check all of them. Anyhow, I can't imagine Mr. Loftman being fool enough to apply for the tickets in his own name. With regards to the letter, all the C.I.B. can tell us was that it was posted at the General Post Office in Sydney. They suggest we get in touch with them if and when you receive any more of these anonymous letters."

"Not very encouraging, is it?" murmured Mr. Palfrey. "It occurred to me after you had gone that the writer of the letter might be in the employ of the lottery people. How else would he know about the sale of lottery tickets to Mr. Loftman?"

"You've got a point there . . ." Zoe said thoughtfully. "I'll ask the C.I.B. to check up on that score. By the way, have there been any more discrepancies?"

"No. Strangely enough, they seem to have stopped."

"Hmmm . . . looks as if Mr. Loft-man has seen the red light."

"Yes . . . I . . . er . . . was wondering whether we ought to go ahead with the investigation in the circum-stances . . ?"

"Oh, come now," Zoe protested, "you can't afford to let things slide in that fashion. After all, you've got no guarantee that he won't help himself again in the very near future. He can grow more ambitious as time

goes by and maybe abscond with a considerable sum. There's no telling what he might get up to!"

"Yes, I suppose you're right . . ." sighed Mr. Palfrey. "It seems such a pity, though. . . He always struck me as being such a steady fellow. I wonder what came over him?"

"He's probably developed some sort of a kink. These elderly introverts tend to go off the rails after a while. With some it's women, with others it's—"

"Yes, well, never mind," Mr. Palfrey put in hurriedly. "Get in touch with me as soon as you find out something definite."

"Would you like Mr. Loftman followed in the meantime?"

"I don't think that will serve any useful purpose at this juncture," he said.

Zoe had to wait another two weeks before the C.I.B. report came through. They apologised for the delay, saying that it had taken them some time to check the handwriting of the persons in the employ of the State Lottery. They regretted to report that they had drawn a blank in that respect. There was, however, an Englishman by the name of Travers, on the clerical staff. He had only been in the country a few months.

"He claims that he was never at any time employed by Messrs. Palfrey, Mason & Wood Ltd. You might care to check with them in the matter," the report concluded. There was a footnote giving a full description of Travers.

Zoe immediately got on the phone to Mr. Palfrey.

"I've just had some interesting news from the C.I.B.," she gave him to understand. "They want to know whether you at any time employed someone by the name of Herbert Travers. His description is as follows: height, five feet seven inches, dark complexion, brown eyes, prominent front teeth and—"

"Never mind about that now," Mr. Palfrey broke in. "Loftman's disappeared."

"Oh . . !" exclaimed Zoe, momentarily taken aback. "I'll be right over."

Mr. Palfrey could not have been more distracted if he had accidentally stumbled across a nudist colony in his own back yard.

"Loftman didn't put in an appearance this morning," he gabbled, ushering Zoe into his office. "I thought perhaps he had been taken ill, so I sent someone round to his flat. He's not there! The caretaker informed the messenger that he hadn't seen Loftman at all over the weekend."

"Have you checked the contents of the safe?" Zoe enquired.

"Not yet. Mr. French is working on it now."

There was an apologetic cough from the direction of the door.

"Come in, French," Mr. Palfrey said impatiently. "What have you found?"

"There's nothing missing, sir. Every penny is accounted for," reported the dapper Mr. French ingratiatingly.

"Who else, besides Mr. Loftman, has a key to the safe?" interposed Zoe, noticing that his left hand was bandaged.

"Only my partners and I," Mr. Palfrey gave her to understand.

"And there's nothing missing . . . that's odd," mused Zoe.

"What do we do now?" Mr. Palfrey wanted to know.

"It's up to you. Do you want me to get in touch with the police?" Zoe asked.

"No. For all we know he may have met with an accident. Perhaps you would be good enough to check with the various hospitals."

"All right," shrugged Zoe, making for the door, "but I have a feeling I shall be wasting my time. By the way, supposing they ask me for a description. He may not have been carrying any means of identification on his person, in which case they will expect me to describe him."

"Yes, of course. Well, he's about 52 years of age, greyish hair, wears glasses and—well, about how tall would you say he was, Mr. French?"

"About six feet, sir."

"As much as that?"

"Well, he has round shoulders, sir, and what with his slight stoop and everything, it makes him look shorter, if you know what I mean."

"How about his style of dress?" Zoe asked.

"Very conservative, Miss," the assistant cashier answered. "Most conservative. Always wore a dark grey stripe—"

"What makes you use the past tense?" Zoe shot at him.

"I'm sorry," apologised the other. "It was just a slip of the tongue."

"Well, I think that will be all for now," Zoe said, bidding them good-morning.

None of the major hospitals were able to assist her in the matter. A surprisingly large number of people had suffered injuries over the weekend, but none of them seemed to answer to Mr. Loftman's description. She tried the morgues next, with no result.

"I'm afraid we've drawn a complete blank," she confessed to Mr. Palfrey over the telephone the following afternoon.

"Oh, dear . . ." murmured Mr. Palfrey.

"What about this Travers person?" Zoe put to him.

"Who?"

"Travers. Herbert Travers. I spoke to you about him over the 'phone yesterday. The C.I.B. want to know whether anyone by that name was at any time employed by you."

"Oh, yes, I remember now. It went clean out of my head. Just a minute while I check with the Personnel manager. . ."

Zoe was able to repair her make-up, and re-varnish her nails during the so-called 'minute'.

"I'm sorry to have kept you waiting," he apologised. "The Personnel manager wasn't in his office. I had to check through the Personnel file myself. There's no one by that name on our files, I'm afraid."

"It's possible that he may have been using another name at the time, or that Travers is an assumed name in this instance," Zoe conjectured. "Tell me, does the following description ring a bell?" she added, repeating the description she had relayed to him over the 'phone the previous morning.

"Projecting teeth . . ." Mr. Palfrey said, after a lengthy pause. "Do you know, I seem to recollect having engaged a temporary clerk at one time or other who answers to the description. I'll check with our Personnel manager as soon as he comes in, and then I'll ring you back."

He failed to keep his word in that respect, and Zoe dropped in to see him the following morning. "You were going to 'phone me," she reminded him.

"So I was!" he said apologetically. "I forgot all about it in the general excitement."

"What excitement?"

"Mr. Loftman's back! It seems he met with an accident. He usually drives over to Windsor most weekends and stays there with some friends. Apparently he was taking a stroll along the river on Sunday night when he was knocked down and robbed by a thief. He was admitted to hospital suffering from concussion. That is why he wasn't able to let us know what happened. He came in this morning with his head all bandaged up. He insisted he was all right, but I sent him home."

"Looks as if we're right back where we started from . . ." mused Zoe. "How about this Travers fellow—you know, the one with the prominent teeth?"

"Oh, yes. I had a word with the

Personnel manager and he tells me that he remembers hiring a temporary clerk some time back, and that the fellow fits the description you gave me, but his name was Turnbull."

"That doesn't mean a thing," replied Zoe. "I think I'll ask the C.I.B. to keep an eye on Mr. Travers. I'll be seeing you."

"One moment!" Mr. Palfrey called after her. "Do you happen to know of a good locksmith?"

"Yes. Why?"

"Well, I'm afraid we'll have to get the lock on the safe changed. You

see, the thug who knocked Mr. Loftman down took everything contained in his pockets, including his keys, one of which fitted the safe."

"Oh, I see. Well, I should get in touch with Mr. Edward Biggs. His telephone number is Clissold 4300," Zoe said, taking her leave.

She received a telephone call from Mr. Palfrey the following morning at a little after ten.

"It's terrible!" he cried hysterically. "You must come over right away!"

"Now, calm down and tell me what's happened," she said soothingly.

"Mr. French, the assistant cashier, has disappeared!"

"Oh, no!" groaned Zoe. "What is this—some sort of a game?"

"Game!" shrieked Mr. Palfrey. "It may interest you to know that he has taken the entire contents of the safe with him! There was over £8,000 in the safe and—"

"Have you notified the police?"

"No. I thought I'd get in touch with you first."

"Ring Scotland Yard and ask to be put through to Detective Sergeant Tweedie," Zoe instructed him. "I'll be over as soon as I can."

Tweedie was already on the job by the time she put in an appearance.

"This is a pretty kettle of fish!" he greeted her severely. "Why weren't we called in right from the start?"

"I did suggest it," Zoe said on the defensive, "but Mr. Palfrey vetoed the idea. How did French manage to get the safe open?" she asked, thinking to change the subject.

"I think I can explain how," Mr. Loftman said from the doorway. "He followed me to Windsor, and attacked me while I was taking a walk down by the river on Sunday night. He deliberately emptied my pockets to make it look as if I'd been knocked down by a thief, when in actual fact all he wanted were the keys to the safe."

"That makes sense," nodded Zoe.

"What infuriates me more than anything else is that the young swine should add insult to injury by stealing my car into the bargain!" Mr. Loftman ground out savagely.

"Really?" exclaimed Zoe.

"Yes," nodded Tweedie. "I've already had a description of it sent out over the teletype. I don't think our friend French is going to get very far."

"Mr. Loftman also has a theory concerning the letter we received from Australia," Mr. Palfrey put in. "I told him about it this morning and—"

"What letter?" Tweedie shot at him.

"We'll explain in a minute," Zoe interposed quickly. "What about this

theory of yours, Mr. Loftman?"

"Well, there was one very obvious clue, in my opinion, as to the identity of the writer. You will remember that he mentions that I'm earning £15 per week. Now, the only members of the firm who know how much my salary is, are Mr. Palfrey, Mr. Mason, Mr. Wood and Mr. French. Obviously none of the directors could have written the letter. Therefore, it must have been French . . ."

"But it was posted in Australia," Zoe put in. "How could he possibly have posted it—unless he had someone out there do it for him!" she added, snapping her fingers. "Why didn't I think of it before! Travers must have posted it for him!"

"I'm not so sure," Loftman said, shaking his head. "You will remember that the address on the envelope was typewritten, whereas the note was written by hand. It's my guess there was a letter from Australia in the mail that morning, and that French steamed it open, removed the contents, replaced it with the letter he had written and resealed the envelope."

"You've missed your vocation, Mr. Loftman," Zoe said admiringly. "You should have gone in for crime detection. What I don't understand, however, are French's motives?"

"He was obviously endeavouring to 'frame' me, as they would say in criminal circles. He must have been

"Let me know if and when you catch up with him," Zoe said to Tweedie on her way out.

"I will," he promised.

He was as good as his word. She found him waiting for her on the doorstep the following morning. "You'll be interested to know that we've found Mr. French," he gave her to understand.

"Well done!" she applauded. "Did he come quietly, as the saying goes?"

"Oh, yes, very quietly. In fact, he couldn't have been quieter."

"What do you mean?"

"I mean that he was dead—burnt to a frazzle, and that goes for the car, too."

"What happened?"

"He must have skidded, and gone off the road. The car ran into a tree and then caught fire. He must have been knocked unconscious and— well, you can imagine the rest."

"Ugh! How horrible!" shuddered Zoe.

"By the way, do you happen to know whether Mr. Loftman happens to have an artificial leg?" Tweedie asked, apropos of nothing.

"Are you joking?" Zoe said, giving him an icy stare. "Because if so, I think it's in extremely bad taste and—"

"No, I mean it. You see, Loftman's car is fitted with a hand clutch, instead of the usual foot variety. We figured that he must have an artificial leg. It's only people with artificial limbs who go to the trouble of having the clutch altered."

"So what?" she shrugged.

"Nothing. Just wondered, that's all."

"What happened to the money— was that burnt, too?" Zoe asked, as he turned to go.

"Looks like it. We found the charred remains of a satchel in the car. I imagine the money was in it."

"Well, that about winds up the case as far as you're concerned, I suppose?"

"Yes. Don't forget to send your

planning this robbery for some time, but before putting it into operation he wanted to make sure that someone else got the blame for it."

"Yes, I think you've got something there . . ." nodded Zoe.

"That's fine!" interjected Tweedie cuttingly. "I'm glad you've worked it all out so neatly between you. And now, if it isn't asking too much, perhaps one of you might care to let me know what this is all about?"

"Well, it's like this," Zoe said, giving him the facts.

"I'm inclined to agree with Mr. Loftman," he announced, having heard her out. "As I said before, I don't think our friend French will get very far."

bill to Messrs. Palfrey, Mason & Wood!" he smiled, tipping his hat.

"I most certainly won't," she said primly. "But before doing so I'm going down to Windsor."

"What on earth for?" he asked, halting in his tracks.

"Wouldn't you like to know!" she called mockingly over her shoulder.

On her return from Windsor she dropped in at the Yard in order to have a word with Tweedie.

"You and I have a date with Mr. Palfrey," she gave him to understand.

"What on earth for?"

"I'll explain on the way down there. You'd better hurry, we haven't much time!"

Mr. Palfrey seemed surprised to see them. "We were just about to close up," he said nervously.

"We shan't keep you very long," Zoe smiled. "Would you mind calling in Mr. Loftman. We'd like a word with him."

The head cashier kept them waiting some minutes before putting in an appearance. "Sorry to keep you waiting," he apologised. "I was right in the middle of a column of figures."

"That's all right," Zoe said smoothly. "There's just a small item we'd like you to clear up for us. Had French ever driven your car before?"

"No, I don't think so . . ." Loftman said cautiously.

"I take it no one in the firm knew about your artificial leg?" Zoe said, trying a different tack.

"Now, look here—!" he burst out furiously.

"What is all this about?" Mr. Palfrey interposed with a certain amount of trepidation.

"Your charming and inoffensive Mr. Loftman happens to be a murderer, that's all," Zoe said grimly. "French couldn't possibly have stolen his car. He had a bad hand, you will remember. It was a physical impossibility for him to have driven a car fitted with a hand clutch. I realised it immediately Tweedie mentioned the clutch to me. It may interest you to know, Mr. Loftman, that I paid a visit to Windsor hospital today. They have no record at all of having admitted you to the hospital. You invented the whole business about French knocking you down and stealing the keys to the safe."

"I still don't understand what this is all about!" cried Mr. Palfrey, clasping his aching head.

"It's all very simple really," Zoe assured him. "French did try to frame him by means of the anonymous letter. He was after Loftman's job, I imagine. Anyhow, someone in the office must have tipped Loftman off about the letter. He put two and two together, and decided that he would turn the tables on French, and at the same time rob the firm of £8,000. He had French meet him somewhere and, having knocked him on the head, he dumped him in the car and set light to it. And there you have it."

"You're mad!" Loftman sneered. "You haven't a shred of evidence—"

"Haven't we?" Zoe countered. "Show him what you've got in that satchel, Tweedie."

Tweedie proceeded to tip a tremendous pile of notes on to the desk.

"I took the liberty of breaking into your flat, Mr. Loftman, on the way over here," Zoe grinned. "We found a parcel stuffed up the chimney, of all places! You'll never guess what it contained!"

"Why, you—" swore Loftman, lunging at her, only to be intercepted by Tweedie.

"Take him away, Tweedie," Zoe said, with an airy wave of her hand. "He's beginning to bore me . . ."

HOBBY HOLIDAYS
Holidays with a difference
HILDA YOUNG HAS SOME SUGGESTIONS FOR YOU

A group of riders set off on a pony trek from Hemsley Youth Hostel in Yorkshire.

Have you ever wished that you had more time to spend on your favourite hobby and also that you knew someone else who shared your enthusiasm for riding . . . cycling . . . walking . . . dancing, and so on?

If you have, why not try a hobby holiday this year, a holiday during which you spend your time enjoying your favourite pursuit, helped by experts, and among new friends who also share your love of that particular pastime.

ADVENTURE ASTRIDE

Most girls have longed at some time in their lives to go riding, and the Youth Hostel Association have a riding course, situated in the Cotswolds, which is ideal for beginners. Girls learn all about horse management and receive expert tuition from experienced staff. A similar holiday can be enjoyed near York, with ample time also to explore this beautiful historic city.

If you feel that you would enjoy pony trekking, then spend a week at the Holiday Fellowship's Glasbury Centre in the Black Mountains. Novices travel along the "smooth" route, but more experienced riders may trek along a route which allows for a controlled canter or gallop.

Ponies are very docile and they vary in size to cater for the different weights of their riders . . . fifteen stone being the maximum weight allowed for a rider!

ON FOOT AND WHEELS

If a cycle is your favourite form of transport, you can tour various parts of England such as Sussex, the Wye Valley, Wales and the Yorkshire Dales, with a small band of fellow-cyclists.

There is plenty of time for sight-seeing as you go along, and the distances travelled daily are only moderate, so are well within the capabilities of any normal girl in good health.

Although it is not essential to have a lightweight bicycle, the one you use *must* be in good condition. There is also a special trophy to be won on these cycling holidays. It is given to the person who, in the opinion of a panel of experts, has contributed most to the spirit of cycle-touring. The winner may hold the trophy for one year.

Among the youth hostels at which you may stay during this holiday are an old coaching inn, a farmhouse in the heart of the Devonshire moors, and one hostel which was once a priory.

But should you wish to spend a walking holiday under similar conditions, you will find this equally enjoyable, visiting famous beauty spots, exploring wild moorlands or fascinating footpaths with an experienced leader. You will munch away at a picnic lunch and then return to the hostel to a hot meal and congenial company, to discuss the day's adventures and plan your routes for the next day.

Remember that strong shoes are essential on a walking holiday, and should you decide on either the Lake District or the High Peak, it would be advisable to have some experience of walking in rough country, or be prepared to practise before you go.

HOLIDAY AFLOAT

One unusual holiday you might like is cruising down some of England's rivers in a canal boat. Each boat carries twelve passengers in dormitory-type accommodation, and you have to bring your own sheets or a sleeping-bag.

The narrow boat is horse-drawn, and if you like you can look after the horse, steer the boat and learn to navigate the locks. If you wish, you can explore some of the places *en route*, and then catch up with the boat later on.

Should you require a more energetic holiday, try a yachting cruise in the Hebrides run by the Holiday Fellowship, or try their Three-in-One holiday,

when a week is spent canoeing, pony trekking and sailing at the Tan Troad Adventure Centre.

The Youth Hostel Association also run a sailing holiday on the River Dart in Devon which is great fun. Expert tuition is given every day in dinghies and there is always a lifeguard in attendance. Life-jackets, which are provided free, must be worn at all times, and anyone taking this holiday *must* be able to swim at least fifty yards.

FLOWERS AND FOLK DANCING

But if your interests are of a quieter nature, such as a love of flowers or folk dancing, you can still enjoy them on holiday.

The Holiday Fellowship Association hold a course at Penzance on floral art for beginners. Here members are shown how to make the best of each season's flowers, to grow their own flowers and to create their own arrangements.

Those wishing to attend this holiday course are asked to bring along a soup-dish, scissors and a plastic bag to collect wild flower material.

If the actual collecting of wild flowers is your hobby, then the holiday on the isle of Arran will prove ideal for you, as it is designed for all those interested in field botany and the study and identification of flowering plants.

At Loch Leven, too, you can enjoy a dancing holiday, where you can have dancing instructions in the morning and then enjoy a series of excursions to places of interest in the afternoons.

All set for a pleasant afternoon's sailing.

Two friends outside the stables at Exford Youth Hostel which is used as a base for pony-trekking holidays on Exmoor.

A similar holiday, this time with folk dancing, can be taken at Scarborough, when you may learn the steps of many European dances, from places as far apart as England and Russia. A resident musician will be in attendance, but if you yourself play an instrument please take it along and help to make more merry music.

These are just a few of the hobby holidays you could take. Others include photography, bird study, painting, freelance writing, archaeology and music. Details of these, together with times and prices, can be obtained from the following addresses:

THE HOLIDAY FELLOWSHIP
142 Great North Way
Hendon
London, N.W.4

YOUTH HOSTEL ASSOCIATION
29 John Adam Street
London, W.C.2

A young onlooker watches a group of canoeists as they guide their craft through grass-lined waters.

From Bedroom to Bedsitter

Have you ever thought how easy it would be to transform that dull, ordinary bedroom, with the pastel flowery paper into a zingy bedsitter? Yes, you have, but it would cost too much? Dad would object? Well, I think the answer to both these problems lies in the way that you tackle things. I should deal with dad first. And you're the expert there—after all, you may have to enlist his help, or at least borrow some of his tools.

Gudrun Heatley suggests ways to transform a dull, ordinary bedroom without involving too much cost.

FIRST THINGS FIRST

When you've been given the go-ahead the first thing to do is to have a good look at your bedroom's assets. It may be a good shape, or have an interesting alcove or a nice window; it's bound to have something on which you can focus interest.

Well, I should imagine that you have a bed, a wardrobe, a dressing-table and a carpet. You've probably also got a whole picture gallery of your favourite pop and film stars. I'm sorry, but they'll have to go, for the time being at least.

A RAZZAMATAZZ OF COLOUR

Choosing your colour scheme is one of the nicest parts of interior decorating; the hard part comes later. Obviously you have favourite colours, but beware: yellow, orange and purple are great in small doses, but just try to imagine your room a riot of colour with these shades. Perhaps one wall, or even two, but remember you're going to spend a lot of time in there. Are you going to like it as much in six months as you do now? Often the best thing to do is to look through a whole host of colour magazines, even the advertisements, because you will be able to get some ideas from here.

Bright, clear, strong colours are the best and remember that they needn't necessarily be vivid. If you like pink—and lots of girls prefer it to the bright purples and yellows—then have pink. But what about trying a deeper, raspberry shade? This looks very nice with perhaps a paler ice-cream shade of pink and splashes of deep blue.

There are some general interior-decorating beliefs which might help you in your choice. For example, bold colours will make a room look smaller,

therefore pale ones are obviously going to make it look larger. A feeling of warmth may be created by using the warmer toned colours, red, yellow, orange and brown, while coolness and peace come with the blues, greens, beiges and white. A word of caution here; do remember that dark colours look even darker over large areas and colours may react violently to their neighbours; so check first. It is usually better to contrast a warm tone with a cooler one.

FABRIC FANFARE

Look for unusual fabrics, both for wall and window coverings. Cork, felt, hessian, they all look great on walls, and the open weave materials which are now on the market look super made up into curtains and coverings. The texture of all these fabrics makes them interesting no matter what colour you choose.

Cork is perhaps the most difficult, because it is not easy to work with and it is also quite expensive. It is, I think,

SIMPLY MADE—BUT VERY EFFECTIVE

Perhaps the carpet isn't what you would have chosen, but you're stuck with it! The best thing to do would be to run your colour scheme with the colour of the carpet in mind and then have one or two rugs to break up the overall effect of the carpet.

But rugs can be very expensive. A very cheap and simple idea is to make your own, and this isn't as hard as you

CURTAIN CHOICE

It is amazing how curtains may change the whole appearance of a room. The only rule here is to choose your length and stick to it! Either short, sill-level curtains, or long, full-length ones, never in between, because all you achieve is a kind of chopped-off look, which isn't at all flattering.

The fabric departments are literally bulging at the seams with all kinds of curtain fabrics and colours. A simple guideline which interior decorators use when planning a room is: something light, something dark, something shiny and something dull. So when you're choosing your wall coverings and colour scheme bear this in mind.

MAKING THE BEST OF WHAT YOU'VE GOT

As I said earlier, it probably isn't possible to start from scratch with your bedroom furniture and it may not be exactly what you would have chosen, but don't despair.

Let's start with your bed. Why not cover your headboard in the same fabric as your curtains. Simply make a flattish cushion, filled with kapok, the same size as the headboard, and use a strong adhesive to stick it on. It is often an idea to dispense with a formal headboard altogether and simply attach a similar padding to the wall, either just at the headboard end or if your bed is pushed up against a wall, on that wall too, so as to give a sitting-area effect.

To carry this idea through, why not make a couple of cushions in the same fabric and then a contrasting bedspread. Either a plain one, picking out one of the main colours in your patterned curtains, or a patterned one which contains the colour of your curtains if they are plain.

Wardrobes, chests-of-drawers and dressing-tables are very difficult to disguise. You could paint them a colour which will tone with the rest of your colour scheme—but do get permission first. It's also fun to decorate this type of furniture with motifs, so that the solid effect of the piece of furniture is broken up.

A few gay posters on your freshly decorated walls and you're on the threshold of a brand-new world. Now you've got a place of your own where you can curl up and relax, do your homework and bring your friends; you've got a room that isn't just a bedroom. And you'll find that interior decorating is lots of fun too!

worth the trouble, however, because it will stop the heat loss from your room and it also has certain sound-muffling qualities, which should please your parents, especially when you have the latest pop records on at full volume.

Both hessian and felt are available in a wide variety of colours and types, and both are very hard wearing. Wallpapers are available in a great assortment of rainbow colours and textures as wallpaper manufacturers become more and more adventurous.

might at first think.

A very simple but colourful rug can be made out of felt. Choose the shape that you would like, and the colour, then cut it out and sew some fringing or perhaps bobbles round the edge, and hey presto! For an even more original finish cut out shapes in contrasting colours and appliqué them to your base. Abstract shapes look best, or simple flower shapes. You can even carry this idea through to a wall-hanging or bedspread.

believe it or not!

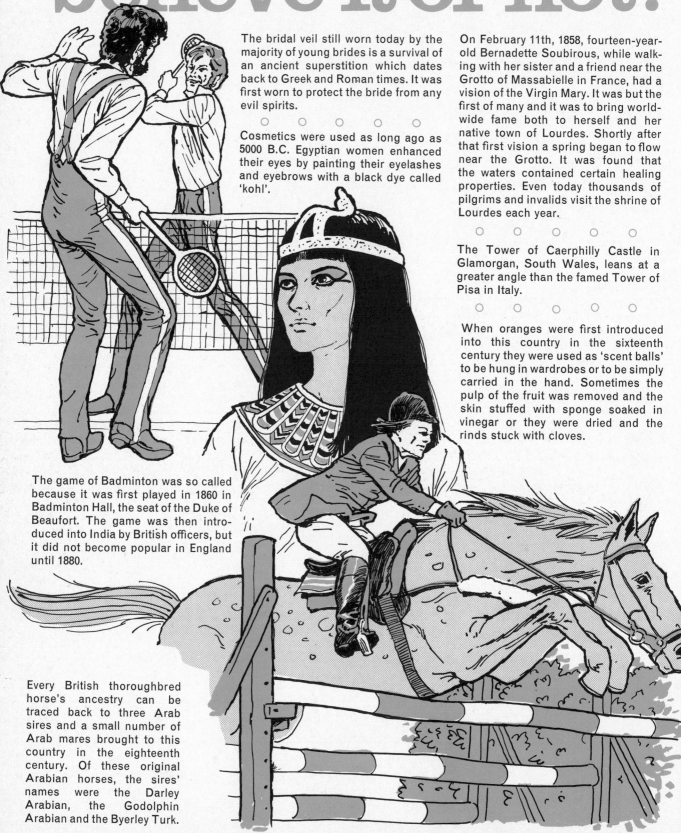

The bridal veil still worn today by the majority of young brides is a survival of an ancient superstition which dates back to Greek and Roman times. It was first worn to protect the bride from any evil spirits.

Cosmetics were used as long ago as 5000 B.C. Egyptian women enhanced their eyes by painting their eyelashes and eyebrows with a black dye called 'kohl'.

On February 11th, 1858, fourteen-year-old Bernadette Soubirous, while walking with her sister and a friend near the Grotto of Massabielle in France, had a vision of the Virgin Mary. It was but the first of many and it was to bring world-wide fame both to herself and her native town of Lourdes. Shortly after that first vision a spring began to flow near the Grotto. It was found that the waters contained certain healing properties. Even today thousands of pilgrims and invalids visit the shrine of Lourdes each year.

The Tower of Caerphilly Castle in Glamorgan, South Wales, leans at a greater angle than the famed Tower of Pisa in Italy.

When oranges were first introduced into this country in the sixteenth century they were used as 'scent balls' to be hung in wardrobes or to be simply carried in the hand. Sometimes the pulp of the fruit was removed and the skin stuffed with sponge soaked in vinegar or they were dried and the rinds stuck with cloves.

The game of Badminton was so called because it was first played in 1860 in Badminton Hall, the seat of the Duke of Beaufort. The game was then introduced into India by British officers, but it did not become popular in England until 1880.

Every British thoroughbred horse's ancestry can be traced back to three Arab sires and a small number of Arab mares brought to this country in the eighteenth century. Of these original Arabian horses, the sires' names were the Darley Arabian, the Godolphin Arabian and the Byerley Turk.

THE HEALING OF THE LAME MAN

Reuben had been born lame. He had never run about, climbed trees or raced in the countryside.

Of course, while his parents were alive they'd done their best—if he'd been born to pagan parents they would have left him somewhere to die. But Reuben's family believed in the one, true God, so that even a lame child was cared for.

But even if they had cared for him they hadn't been able to make him whole, so he'd spent his days lying or sitting on his mattress, helping where he could in a few household tasks, small things he could manage from his mattress.

But now he was old.

"And there is no one to care if I live or die," he thought.

Then he scolded himself. "Haven't you some of the finest friends a man may have?" he told himself. "Don't they carry you each day to the Temple, that you may beg where all the world passes by?"

He reclined there, on his mat, with his earthenware bowl by his side, and the cheerful farewells of his friends ringing in his ears.

A story from the Bible retold by Katherine M. McLean

He was very fortunate to be here, he reminded himself. Didn't he love the Temple Courts? If only he could join the men in the Court of the Israelites!

Still, he was near the Beautiful Gate—and very, very beautiful it was!

It was too beautiful to look at when the sunshine glinted on it—and indeed the Corinthian brass, more costly than gold or silver, made you shut your eyes and turn away from the brilliance.

It was so massive that it required a staff of twenty men to close it each evening and roll it back each morning.

It led into the Court of the Gentiles, where people of any nationality might enter. Beyond was a wall on which tablets were set, warning that a Gentile would pass beyond this spot at his peril; death would follow.

up with it! But it's not right to keep animals here, in God's house.

Today seemed bad from the start.

Then, suddenly, Reuben saw two men come near. They often went into the Temple. They'd been friends of that man Jesus and had since formed a band which went about preaching.

He leaned forward and held out his bowl.

"Alms, give alms," he cried.

The two men stopped. Peter looked at John and then back at the beggar.

"I have no gold or silver," began Peter.

Reuben sank back.

Well, if they hadn't—they hadn't. It was just one of those days.

But Peter and John didn't pass by.

"Look on us," said Peter.

Surprised, the lame man obeyed.

He saw the loving kindness and pity in the men's eyes, and a light of great power.

"I have no gold or silver," repeated Peter, "but what I have, I will give to you."

He took the lame man's hand.

"In the name of Jesus Christ of Nazareth, rise up and walk!" he cried.

Reuben stared, and then new life seemed to run through his veins as Peter pulled him to his feet. A new strength surged through his bones as, tremblingly, he stood—stood for the first time in all his life!

Oh, the wonder! Oh, the wonder!

Then, full of joy, he leaped and ran, shouting his praise and thanks.

"Let me come with you into the Temple," he cried, following the two men.

Crowds gathered, running after the three.

As they reached Solomon's Porch, Peter turned and spoke to the mob.

"Don't marvel, or look at us as if we have worked wonders by our own skill or holiness," he said. "It is through the power of Jesus, whom you crucified, that we do these things."

You may read the whole of this wonderful story—and what happened next, in the Acts, chapters 3 and 4.

Reuben had a good position for begging, but he knew only too well that many of the worshippers would turn the other way, pretending not to see him or to hear his cry: "Alms, give alms."

Yes, he found much to watch.

There were the pompous businessmen, fat from good living and full of their own importance; the ordinary folk intent on praising their God; the little widow woman who gave all that she possessed—a single coin worth little compared with the silver tossed in by the rich, who didn't even miss their offering.

Sometimes Reuben would hear the distant music of the choirs. He would see the smoke of incense rise to the blue sky, for the Temple Courts had no roofs.

But there were the bad days, when feet shuffled by and men did not cast even the smallest coin into his bowl; when the shouts of the merchants at their stalls and tables in the Court of the Gentiles were noisier than ever, and when the smell of the sacrificial animals could hardly be borne. . . . Though, thought Reuben, with a grin, a man in my position must put

The GIRL FROM CONCORD
the story of the real Jo March

The Alcott family of Concord, Massachusetts, were returning home from an afternoon walk, when suddenly Bronson Alcott missed his young daughter, Louie. Hearing a cry of fright from the direction of a woodland pond, Mr. Alcott raced down a slope, and was just in time to see a young coloured boy drag Louie, wet and bedraggled, safely back to shore.

"Louie, Louie, I thought you had learnt your lesson when you got lost as a toddler in the ship's engine-room, and led your mother and I such a dance before we found you," chided her father as he wrapped her in his coat and carried her home. "I wish you would channel your energy into more sensible fields of activity. After all, you are getting quite a young lady now."

Louie took her father's words to heart, and decided to concentrate on trying to produce some saleable stories to help the family's finances. She enjoyed writing, and although her father was an excellent teacher he had very progressive ideas on education for the mid-nineteenth century, and as a result the family were poor.

But Louie was very proud of her father, and when she started a school for poor children in a barn, to earn a little more money, she tried to teach them as her father had taught her three sisters, Lizzie, May, Anna, and herself, and was delighted when the children began to read and write, and think and act sensibly for themselves.

Among her father's friends were many famous writers and poets, including David Thoreau and Ralph Waldo Emerson. The latter helped and encouraged Louie in her literary ambitions, and it was for Emerson's small daughter that Louie wrote a collection of short stories. She read these to the child while their elders chatted about topics of the day, and so prevented the little girl from being bored.

Later, to Louie's great delight, these were accepted by a publisher under the title *Flower Fables*.

Louie was a great admirer of Florence Nightingale, having read her *Notes on Nursing*, and when the Civil War broke out in 1861, Louie offered her services as a nurse in Washington. Although she worked long, hard hours she still found time to write home to her family about all that went on in the hospital. Her letters home were used as a basis for her *Hospital Sketches*, which was published in 1863.

Louie was now turning out dozens of stories, all of which sold, and she was happy to provide her father and sisters with many small luxuries which they had once been unable to afford.

Then, one day, when she visited her publisher in his office, he made a surprising request. He asked Louie to write a story for him about a typical American family.

Louie was completely dismayed at the idea, for she was a spinster of 36. But as she walked home, she started to recall the happy days of long ago when she and her sisters were small. "I will write a story about us," she thought, as she hurried along the crowded pavements.

Incidents came crowding back to her and she could hardly wait to get them down on paper. The Alcotts became the March family, poor like the proverbial church mice, because Father was away in Washington and Marmee and the girls had to manage on very little money.

The March girls themselves were Louie's own sisters; delicate Lizzie became Beth, her name only changed in form; Anna, who always hated being poor, became sweet-tempered Meg, and May's name was rearranged to become Amy, golden-haired, and always worrying about altering the shape of her nose. Louie herself was tomboy Jo, who befriended Laurie, the rich, but lonely, boy next door, grandson of crusty, but kind-hearted, Mr. Lawrence.

Into her story Louie wove several half-forgotten events which would have lain dormant forever if circumstances had not forced her memory to recall them. The sisters performed a play called the *Witch's Curse*, which had been specially written by Jo to revive her spirits because it was to be another Christmas without presents.

Then there was the day that Jo, trying to be more lady-like, invited Laurie to a tea party, at which everything went wrong.

The last straw came when Jo saw Laurie pulling strange faces as he ate a dish of strawberries and cream, and discovered to her horror that the cream had turned sour!

But a happier incident was the day Beth received a piano of her very own, a generous gift from Mr. Lawrence, who loved Jo's shy little sister and had often invited her over to his house to play the piano, for they were both extremely fond of music.

Then there was the amusing incident of Amy trying to change the shape of her nose with a peg, and almost losing her breath as a result!

Louie recalled ruefully the time Jo was caught reading a novel instead of the book Aunt March had given her, when the old lady was asleep, and as a punishment was forced to read a tale of missionary activities in far-off lands.

Louie finished the manuscript in ten weeks and, giving it the title *Little Women*, the name bestowed on the Alcott sisters by their father, handed it over, rather hesitantly, to her publisher. He was rather disappointed in the story but, wishing to be quite sure before turning it down, he gave it to his small daughter to read.

The result was simply amazing. The girl curled up in a large armchair with the book, and soon became oblivious to her surroundings. She seemed to resent being called down to meals, and her father was amazed to see tears rolling down her cheeks at one point.

"What is wrong, my love?" he asked anxiously.

"Jo has cut off her lovely hair and sold it to raise money for her mother to visit her father who is sick in far-away Washington!" sobbed the child.

The publisher was amazed, and said to his wife: "She speaks as if they are real people."

His wife assured him that she had heard their daughter laughing at the jokes Jo and Laurie played on each other. When she came to the end of the book at last, the little girl asked her father to bring her more of the adventures of the March family.

Convinced at last that he would be foolish not to publish the book, the publisher sent it off to the printers as quickly as he could. It sold out very swiftly, and young readers wrote to Louie demanding to be told more of the March family.

Bowing to popular demand, the curtain now rose on the later years of the March girls. Unfortunately, delicate Beth was lost to the readers, but Meg, Amy and even tomboy Jo eventually married and became *Good Wives*.

Meg, who had married John Brook, had twins, Daisy and Demi; Amy caused a surprise by marrying Laurie, and Jo found lasting happiness with Professor Bhaer.

Later, in *Jo's Boys* and *Little Men*, Louie told of the trials and light-hearted crises which occurred when Jo and her husband turned Plumfield, a large house left to them by sharp-tempered Aunt March, into a loving home for orphaned and maladjusted boys.

Louie never married, but she spent her life happily writing, travelling and paying long visits to her family.

Her books have been translated into almost every language in the world and at least four versions of *Little Women* have been made for the cinema, a fact which would have delighted, but probably surprised, the modest girl from Concord.

bush baby

by Stephanie Andrews

Life in the outback was hard, but Ann was a Bush Baby and she gloried in the freedom and challenge of it.

Ann Springs stood on the river bank with her back to the water. She could not see the five thousand stampeding horses beyond the hills, but she could hear their pounding hoofs, like the distant rumble of an approaching thunderstorm. Soon they would come charging into sight. Wild with thirst from the dry and dusty outback, they would charge over her and trample her into the dust. The leaders would carry on for the river, would sink in the soft mudbanks, and would be trampled down by the following horses in a massive pile-up.

Ann stood her ground. She wondered if this would be the last Australian sunset she would see. She wondered if she would ever see her parents again. She thought that her end was near, but she was grateful that she had had fifteen years of happiness. Nothing could take them away from her. Ann uncoiled her stockwhip and waited.

It had all started when the bush fire had swept through the North Territory of Australia on to her father's outback station, where they bred horses. Ann and her mother were almost exhausted by carrying buckets of water to her father and Jet Stone, their aboriginal stockman, who poured the water over the roof of their wooden homestead. Already the flames had caught the dry stubble of their station, and a wall of fire

swept towards them like a tidal wave. Their five hundred and seventeen horses bolted for safety.

"That's all we have time for now," said Mr. Springs, dropping from the roof. "Get inside the house quickly, Ann. You too, Maria. Come on, Jet, get down from that roof. Do you want to fry?"

Ann felt a blast of hot air on her body before she charged into the house. The others followed her and slammed the door after them.

"Get under the table, all of you," yelled Mr. Springs. "Hurry up. If we don't time this properly, we'll all go up in smoke."

The wall of fire wrapped around the house and the walls were engulfed in flames. The timber boards crackled like dry firewood, and a window-frame fell out to let in a blast of hot air and smoke. Ann's father tightened his wet neckerchief over his face. The roof creaked and partially collapsed; burning beams and rafters fell on the floor and table.

"Right, follow me, if you can," said Mr. Springs. He ran to the burning door and tried to pull it open. "Heck, it's jammed," he yelled, and he charged at it with his shoulder.

The door collapsed under his weight, and he was outside. Like a greyhound released from a trap, Ann sprinted after him. Once outside, she could see that the wall of fire had swept away to the other side of the station, leaving the earth bare, black and smoky. But the house was burning furiously.

As the roof fell in, Mr. Springs dashed back to rescue the others. As he was leading them out, a burning joist fell on his shoulder and pinned him to the ground. He screamed out in agony, but Jet, with his bare hands, lifted up the burning joist so that the others could pull him away to safety.

Mrs. Springs dressed her husband's burns in silence. There was no need for anyone to say they had lost their home, their new paddock and entire stock of young horses, in fact everything they possessed.

Mr. Springs coughed. "We'll have to sell this land for what it's worth," he croaked. "Maybe I can find work elsewhere, say in Darwin. Maybe we can start up a riding school for the posh city kids there."

"What are you talking about?" said Mrs. Springs impatiently.

"What am I talking about? What are *you* talking about, you mean!

Don't you realise we are ruined? Even if we could find some of our lost stock, we could never rebuild the station and repay the mortgage we owe."

"Ah, lie still and shut up," said Mrs. Springs. "You can get up when the flying doctor tells you."

"Flying doctor, eh? We won't see much of him. He'll have plenty to do without seeing us."

"He'll be right along after the fire. You've got to give him credit for having some brains, more brains than you'll ever have."

"Brains, ha!"

Mrs. Springs turned on her daughter. "And what are you gawking at?" she snapped. "Don't just sit there like a contented little koala. Go and help Jet tidy up the station. Make yourself useful, if you know how."

Ann shrugged her shoulders and walked off. She knew it was useless arguing with her mother in that mood.

Not that there was much Ann could do. She went down to the river to collect a bucket of water which she thought would be useful and there, in the shelter of the ravine, she saw a herd of wild, but exhausted, horses. None of the horses belonged to her father's herd, unfortunately. On the whole they were a mangy lot, but she could see the herd leader was very different. Ann had an eye for horses, and she recognised the leader as a fine specimen, by any standards.

"*Whoa*, boy, *whoa*," she said softly, as she approached him cautiously. Using all her talent as a horsewoman, she reached him without frightening him away, and stroked his neck. "*Whoa*, boy, *whoa*."

Ann's heart was thumping wildly, but she plucked up her courage and swung herself up on to his back. Immediately, the horse bucked and kicked, then he galloped away across the plain, with Ann clinging on to his flying mane. It was quite incredible where he got his energy, especially after fleeing with his herd before the fire.

After a furious five-mile gallop, they approached a long up-rising, and the horse slowed and finally stopped. Ann sighed and relaxed.

"*Wow!*" she gasped. "I thought you were taking me to Queensland. You are as wild as the bush fire. I don't suppose you've got a name, so I'll call you Flame. Come on, Flame, I'll take you home now."

As Ann rode Flame back to her homestead, she had an idea he might be useful when they started up a

riding school in Darwin. She was careful to lock him up securely in a makeshift paddock for the night. Then, thoroughly exhausted herself, she slept under the stars beside him.

The next morning she was up with the dawn. Flame's old fury had returned, and when she mounted him he tossed with rage and Ann had to gallop him all over the territory to break him in. But Flame was eventually mastered.

Mrs. Springs had salvaged what she could from the smouldering ruins of their home and had set up a make-shift camp. Mr. Springs had not helped much, for his injury turned out to be much worse than any of them imagined, so he spent much of his time in a shelter Jet had rigged up for him. After breakfast, Ann and Jet, double-mounted on Flame, set out to recover what they could find of their missing herd.

Acting on information received from wandering aborigines, they found their missing horses mingled with Flame's herd of wild horses, as well as with herds from neighbouring stations.

Ann estimated that there were five thousand head at least, but as Flame was the natural leader of the wild herd she believed that she could get him to bring them all back to Flintstone Valley which, fenced at both ends, would hold them until they were sorted out and reclaimed by their owners.

"Jet," she said, "pick yourself a horse from the herd and head for Flintstone Valley. Fence up the ends to hold the horses. I'll give you an hour, then I'll bring them along if I can."

"Sure, Miss Ann," said Jet in his deep voice. "But bring them into the valley slow and careful, for them horses can be plenty mad."

"I'll see what I can do, but I wish Dad was here to help. I've never handled five thousand horses before."

Jet grinned. "You'll do all right, Miss Ann."

Jet scrambled down into the valley, found his horse and galloped away to fence in the valley. After a while, Ann cracked her stockwhip to move the herd to the pre-arranged corral.

As it turned out, she had less difficulty than he feared, for, before she reached Flintstone Valley, she was joined by stockmen from neighbouring stations who helped her to drive the herd along. Jet had also been helped to fence in the valley enclosure. The stockmen knew exactly what to do, and when they drove in the herd, they closed the gap in the fencing to secure the stock. It had been so smooth an operation that Ann marvelled that it seemed to have been done in such a short

The stockmen were well aware of the dangers. "If they break through the fence and stampede to the river, they'll kill themselves in the rush," said Mr. Crawford.

"*If* they break out?" said a stockman. "You mean *when* they break out. They're wild with thirst. I'm surprised they haven't already broken out. We'd better let a few of them out at a time, before the whole lot panic. We haven't much time."

"Get the stockmen mounted."

The stockmen mounted and opened a narrow exit in the far fence of the valley. Immediately the herd surged forward and trampled down the fence, in spite of the efforts of the stockmen to drive them back.

"The herd's broken out. We can't hold them. They're stampeding!"

It looked as if all of Ann's work had been in vain. She knew she must save the herd at all costs, if she could. She leapt upon Flame's back, not knowing exactly what she could do. She had only a vague plan in the back of her mind. She thought she might get between the herd and the river, and somehow drive them back.

Ann guided Flame along the short cut to the river, over the ridge, but otherwise gave him his head.

Flame, maddened by the sweet smell of water, galloped like the wind. After five miles, Flame was sweating profusely, and Ann slowed him down near the dangerous river bank, slipped off his back and let him pick his own way down the mudbank to the water, to quench his thirst.

Ann stood with her back to the river and licked her dry lips. She felt the hard ground tremble with the thundering of hoofbeats. Then, suddenly, in a distant cloud of dust, she saw the herd. She twitched her stockwhip. She stood her ground. She knew horses were terrified of humans on foot, and she hoped their craze for water would not overcome their fear of her.

As the herd approached, she cracked her stockwhip. The leaders slowed down, giving the stockmen, who were coming up on the flanks, the opportunity to move between the herd and the river.

time. But, in fact, Ann had worked very hard throughout the day, and she was surprised when she realised it was almost sundown.

The stockmen set up a camp in the valley.

"How did you fare in the bush fire, Ann?" asked Mr. Crawford, a neighbouring station owner.

"We lost everything, just about. My dad says he'll have to sell up the land and move out to Darwin. How did you fare?"

"We all lost," said her neighbour. "Some more than others, but we all lost. I didn't do too badly, myself, but we've all got you to thank for saving our herds. If your dad *is* selling, we'll club together to buy his land. We'll see he gets a fair price. That's the least we can do for you."

"Thanks, Mr. Crawford, but you know my dad won't accept charity."

"That's not charity, and I'll tell the stubborn old fool so. It's a fair price for what you did for us, and he can't disagree with that."

Ann yawned. "Well, you'll have to make him the offer yourselves. As you say, he can be stubborn."

Ann was tired after her day's work, and she was almost ready to turn in when she noticed that the wind had changed. Flame's nostrils twitched. The horses in the enclosure were restless. They whinnied and pawed the dusty ground. Ann knew that they had caught the scent of fresh water from the river five miles away.

"The herd is restless," she said. "They can smell the water."

The thirsty herd spread out along the river bank. Only horses in small groups were allowed to pass the line of stockmen to the river. Horses which herded together in larger groups were quickly broken up before they could harm themselves.

So the horses picked their way through the mudbanks to the water. Some of them slithered in the soft mud near the water's edge, but as they were not crowded, they were not trampled underfoot, and were able to pick themselves up. Eventually the whole herd was watered, cooled and calm.

"They'll give us no more trouble now, Mr. Crawford," said Ann.

"Well, little lady," said Mr. Crawford, "I'm at a loss for words. The way you handle horses is . . . is fair dinkum. I know this part of Aus-tralia is home for you, and neither you nor your folks are going to enjoy working in the big city, so this is what me and my neighbours have decided to do. We are not going to make an offer for your dad's land, but we are going to his place, to help rebuild your home and get your dad back on his feet."

"Now you're talking, Mr. Craw-ford," grinned Ann.

Leaving a few of the stockmen to look after the herd, Ann and her neighbouring station-owners rode across to the Springs' station. Mr. Springs was at last up and about. His burns had been heavily bandaged, but he was doing what he could to tidy up his place.

He listened in silence to his neigh-bour's offer of help to rebuild his station, then he exploded.

'Who said I was going to find work in Darwin?" he barked angrily "And why are you wasting your time here now with all this fancy talk of rebuilding houses. We've got five thousand horses by the river. Don't you know prices will be sky-high in Brisbane? We need every man we've got to drive the herd to market before herds from other states move in. When we get back, we can rebuild McClusky's property, then Jacob's then Harrison's, then mine."

Mr. Springs pulled himself on to his horse. It was obvious that his burns still hurt him, but he would allow no one to help him. "Well, what are you waiting for? Pack up your swag. Let's be on our way. You too, Ann. You've got to be more than a pretty face in this territory. It's time you earned your keep."

The drovers moved to the back and to the flanks of the herd. As Flame was still the natural leader of the herd, Ann was allowed to lead the herd across the outback. It was over eight hundred miles to the big city. In a way she regretted that she would not be part of a new, fancy riding school, but on reflection, she knew that she preferred the wild outback life under the stars of the Southern Cross.

framed in beauty

Round metal frames added to a very unusual bridge make these glasses an ideal choice for any fashion-conscious miss.

What is your first reaction when you are told that you need to wear glasses? Dismay . . . resignation . . . or perhaps a secret feeling that you will no longer appear as pretty or attractive as you did without them?

It really is surprising how many girls still experience these typical reactions, even after seeing such famous beauties as Sophia Loren, Princess Farah of Persia and Princess Grace of Monaco wearing glasses, and looking even more charming than they did before.

Choose With Care

The secret of success with glasses is to choose them with as much care as you would a dress or suit or an important accessory, taking into consideration your colouring and face-shape, for frames are as close to your skin as your cosmetics, and as much a part of you as your smile or your voice.

Your frame colour should blend with your hair, complexion and eyes, while the outline of the frame should be chosen to complement the shape of your face.

Face-shapes

So first of all decide, honestly, the shape of your face. If it is round, have shallow lenses with frames hinged high and wide, to give your face length, but if you have a square face choose lower, lightweight rims to soften your facial outline, never an upswept frame.

Lightweight lower rims are also ideal for anyone with a slender face, together with a very delicate type of frame with a fairly straight browline and a fine bridge, while an oval-shaped face benefits greatly from frames with lots of curve, and a browline flowing upwards.

Your Colour Scheme

Now that you have chosen your frames, what colour shall they be? There are many different shades to choose from, but try and choose one which will enhance your natural colouring.

You probably fall into one of the following categories: blonde, brown-ette, brunette or titian, and most opticians have a colour chart showing you the best tints to choose for your hair colouring.

Brownettes are offered a choice of reds, greens or blues, and brunettes find that similar colours in slightly richer tones are ideal for them. Blondes receive admiring compliments if their frames are in gold or pale pastel shades, as do any red-haired beauties who may also include a darkish mauve in their colour list.

And everyone can wear tortoise-shell frames in patterns of palest yellow and russet, ranging through to deepest amber and richest bronze.

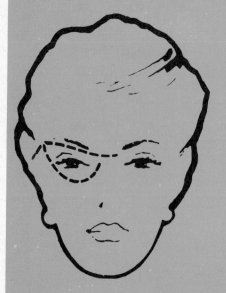

If your face is oval try a frame with plenty of curve and a browline flowing upwards.

A round face needs to be given added length with frames which have sides hinged high and wide, and with shallow lenses.

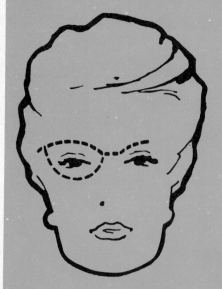

Never have an upswept frame if your face is square; instead have top and lower rims with a slight curve.

A slender face needs a fine bridge, delicate frame and a fairly straight brow-line.

Glasses care

If you take good care of your glasses you will also preserve their efficiency. When a 'wet clean' is required always use the special fluid obtainable from the optician, and never breathe on the lenses before cleaning, as any grit on the glasses would then stick to the lens and, when polishing is com- menced, could scratch the glasses very badly. Always polish with a chamois-leather, real silk or velvet square supplied by the optician, and always replace your glasses in your case when not in use; leaving them face-downwards on a table will soon get them scratched or dimmed.

Glasses for the Sun

But even those of us who do not need glasses for everyday wear eagerly don tinted ones when the sun shines to protect our eyes from its harsh glare. But, never wear cheap sunglasses for long periods at a time, as they do more harm than good.

There are over seventy varieties of tinted lenses available and for normal glasses-wearers their ordinary glasses may be tinted to prevent glare and yet still give them their normal sight, thus eliminating the old-fashioned shades which were once worn over normal lenses.

Colour is a matter of personal choice, but the wise girl always seeks professional advice. Some lenses absorb only infra-red, others only ultra-violet, while some absorb both, but only up to a certain point. Popular anti-glare tints cut down the light by half. In a polarised lens the lens filters out reflected glare by admitting light waves travelling in one direction only.

The newest 'in' thing in the way of sunglasses is the all-in-one-frame-cum-hairband.

So take heart, you short-sighted girls, choose your glasses with care and become a 'framed beauty' of the twentieth century.

Although still keeping the huge round-eye shape, this sunglasses frame has skilfully laminated duotones in which the semi-transparent pearl effect lends depth and dimension to the base colours.

Polished white metal and jet plastic combine to produce glasses with a really slim-rim look.

ROUND THE WORLD

Let's take a magic carpet ride around the world and drop in on many of the colourful festivals which take place in different countries at every season of the year.

AT FESTIVAL TIME

FOLKLORE AND CUSTOMS IN BRITAIN

Britain delights her own folk and visitors alike with the many customs and festivals which take place on these shores each year, bringing excitement and colour to many towns and villages.

They include the Rushbearing Ceremony at Grasmere, in the Lake District; well-dressing at Buxton and other Derbyshire towns, where wells are decorated with Biblical scenes made up entirely of flowers; merrymaking in the streets of Padstow when the Mayday hobbyhorse appears, and countless celebrations in honour of local literary people, such as the Shakespeare festival at Stratford-on-Avon and the Dickens festival at Broadstairs.

North of the border in Scotland there is first-footing on New Year's Eve, the Highland Games at Braemar at which tossing the caber and throwing the hammer are just two of the events which thrill the thousands of spectators, and the Edinburgh Festival of music and drama.

Music-lovers flock also to the International Musical Eisteddfod at Llangollen, in Wales, for a feast of music, dancing and poetry and to see the moving ceremony of *the chairing of the bard*, the acknowledged best poet of that year.

Past meets present during the Dickens Festival at Broadstairs in Kent.

Morris Men delight the crowds at Llangollen with their colourful display of dancing.

SPRING IN SWITZERLAND

Each year in April, in Zurich, spring makes a triumphant return, banishing winter, amid great rejoicing during the *Sechseläuten* or "Six o'Clock Bells", festival. It dates back to Roman times when on the eve of the spring full moon an old man clad in winter furs was led through the streets and thrashed with long, white staves.

Later, in the golden age of Switzerland, the burghers decreed that the cathedral bells were to ring out at the spring equinox, announcing a time of feasting for masters and journeymen.

Today this spring festival is the highlight for young and old alike, but it is a special treat for the children, as on the first day of this popular two-day festival there is a delightful children's parade. Children of every age dress up either in costumes of a bygone age, as various local tradesmen, or as people from other nations of the world.

The following day a banquet is held in many of the guildhalls before the children assemble once more and, accompanied by the *guildsmen* in the colourful historical costumes march to a huge green square called *Alter Tonhalleplatz*. Here, Old Man Winter in a black top hat, and with fireworks hidden about his clothes, sits on his funeral pyre.

On the stroke of six, the first match is put to the pyre and as the *Boögg* burns merrily, the costumed riders of the "Guild of the Camel" gallop madly round this fiery spectacle, to the cheers of the onlookers. Afterwards the merrymaking continues far into the night until, at last, all is over for another year.

A group of dainty little ladies pause to chat during the Zurich Spring Festival.

FOLKLORE FESTIVAL IN MARRAKESH

For anyone who loves music and dancing a visit to the annual folklore festival, at Marrakesh, is a "must" while on holiday in Morocco. All the tribes of the kingdom come to portray their ancient tribal lore in music, song and dance.

Set against the background of the El Bedi Palace, the performers include the heavily bejewelled Ait Hadidou women in their striped cloaks, and Taskiouine dancers who clap their hands and make a great noise on their percussion instruments. One very spectacular dance which delights the audience is the unusual Tissint dagger dance which is performed by men and women together.

The band of musicians add an extra touch of magic to the spectacular danse ahouach *performed by the women of their tribe.*

FUN IN JAPAN

Japan abounds in colourful festivals, in fact there is scarcely a month of the year in which there is not some special reason for merrymaking.

In January Japanese children celebrate their "festival of festivals". This is the name they give to their New Year's Day celebrations, when streets are decorated with plum branches, pine twigs, bamboo stalks and paper garlands.

Later in the month, children in northern Japan build igloos in honour of the Water God and entertain their friends at parties inside these enchanting little snow houses.

Girls like to show off their collections of ceremonial dolls on March the third, while large dolls are made by clever gardeners and florists in October when the Chrysanthemum Dolls Festival is held.

In August in Aomori an old legend is recalled when the festival of Nebuta Matsuri is celebrated. Papier-mâché figures of people, animals and birds, known as *nubuta* are pulled along the streets, re-enacting an old ruse which was used some twelve centuries ago, when a cunning old warrior used a similar trick to outwit his enemies and make them think he had more forces than he actually had.

A large dragon heads the festivities during the October festival of Okunchi Matsuri in the exotic city of Nagasaki, followed by floats and palanquins of every shape, size and colour.

MIDSUMMER NIGHT IN FINLAND

The Finns, too, are very fond of holding festivals, and one of their favourite celebrations is on Midsummer Eve.

Bonfires are lit and there is folk dancing in the streets to celebrate the midnight sun, and in the Aland Islands there is a maypole dance, with each of the dancers wearing colourful national costume.

A very amusing festival is held at Naantali, near Turku, late each July, when because of an old legend everyone must be awake by six o'clock in the morning. Anyone who oversleeps receives a ducking, prizes are given for the best costumes in a colourful procession and dancing starts at dawn and continues to the early hours of the next morning.

This is also the month in which the Aleksis Kivi festival is held near Helsinki. Kivi was a famous Finnish playwright of the last century, and his two most famous plays, *Seven Brothers* and *The Village Cobbler*, which are full of humour, are performed in the open air in the immediate vicinity of Kivi's birthplace.

People ashore and afloat gather to watch the burning of the traditional Midsummer bonfire in Finland.

LUCIA DAY IN SWEDEN

A very fascinating festival takes place each year on the 13th December in Sweden. Known as the "Festival of Lights", it recalls an ancient legend which tells how St. Lucia appeared at Värmland on the darkest night of the year, with a ship full of food to end a great famine there and also bringing with her the precious gift of light.

Now each St. Lucia's Day a pretty fair-haired maiden, dressed in white and wearing a leafy crown decorated with lighted candles, visits each member of her family offering them coffee and specially made "Lucia rolls" to commemorate Lucia's visit and the two gifts which she brought to Sweden so long ago.

Wearing her crown of lighted candles the "Queen of Lights" begins her visits to her family, offering them refreshment.

KERRY'S ROSE OF TRALEE FESTIVAL

With true Irish hospitality Kerry welcomes friends and strangers alike to its late summer festival, where the highlight of the six days of merrymaking is the choosing of the "Rose of Tralee".

The winner is required to have the qualities of the original Rose of Tralee, whose story has become famous throughout the world since William Pembroke Mulchinock composed his well-known ballad. Although the "Rose" need not actually live in Ireland, she must be of Irish origin, and girls have come from as far as Australia, New Zealand and the United States to try to win the coveted title.

The Kerry festival also includes such entertaining attractions as Irish folk groups, floral float parades, ballad competitions, donkey racing, an open-air circus and a veteran car rally.

Folk dancing in the streets during the Rose of Tralee Festival in County Kerry.

91

SINTERKLAAS TIME IN HOLLAND

On the 5th December, Sinterklaas Eve in Holland, the good Bishop Nicholas, in red mitre and mantle with his golden crosier in his hand, comes with his grinning Moorish servant, Black Pieter, to punish or reward children.

Pieter takes the hay left in the wooden shoes for their horses, and in return fills the sabots with sweets, and fills baskets full of presents and leaves them secretly on the doorstep. Sometimes he playfully taps a child with his birch rod, warning him to be good.

Meanwhile every household also wraps up presents, accompanied by mocking little notes, supposedly written by Sinterklaas. These are opened later as the family enjoy a traditional meal which includes *speculaas*, a type of gingerbread, and large chocolate initials which mark each person's place at table.

Black Pieter helps Santa Claus distribute his gifts in Holland.

FAIRYTALE TIME IN DENMARK

Each year in July and August in Odense, the birthplace of Hans Christian Andersen, a festival of the plays of that wonderful storyteller is produced.

Freddy Albeck, the well-known actor, usually plays the part of Andersen, and the children of Odense have great fun acting in the plays. These include *The Tinder Box* about the adventures of the bold soldier, *The Little Mermaid* who exchanged her voice for a pair of legs instead of her fishy tail, and *Simple Simon* who has a series of amusing adventures with a goat. In this latter play the boy playing Simon and the goat, which has an important part in the play, spend the winter really getting to know each other and become firm friends.

The bold soldier meets the witch on his way to seek fame and fortune: a scene from one of the Odense Festival plays. Odense was the birthplace of Hans Andersen.

FAIRS AND FESTIVALS IN INDIA

One of India's most colourful festivals, which lasts ten days, is Dussehra, which is celebrated under different names and in different ways according to the various regions.

In northern India this takes the form of plays, recitations and music about the lives of the legendary hero, Rama, and his wife Sita.

In Delhi the festival is called Ram Lila, and on the last day of the festival immense effigies of Ravana, his brother and his son—which have secretly been filled with fireworks—are taken out to the Ram Lila Grounds where they explode to the cheers of an admiring crowd.

On the last day in Bengal, where the festival becomes Durga Puja, similar images of the warrior-goddess are taken in procession and immersed in the sea or a river.

A feature of Navaratri, as the festival is celebrated in the south, is the tiers of dolls and trinkets which are arranged by young girls, and the many visits exchanged by families and friends.

Often a sidelight to the festivals are the many fairs also held in India. These include cattle fairs at which prizes are awarded for the best cattle. But the most colourful fair of all is held at Pushkar, which includes camel-riding among its many entertainments.

One of the most boisterous of all the festivals is that of the feast of Holi, when everyone—men, women and children—revel in throwing coloured powder and squirting coloured water over their many friends.

At the Indian festival of Holi children delight in squirting water at each other.

The High Priestess holds aloft the flaming torch before it is sent on its long journey to the site of the Olympic Games.

THE OLYMPIC TORCH IN GREECE

Greece has many interesting festivals, including the blessing of the waters at Epiphany, the Mock Peasant Wedding at Thebes and the Flower Festival at Athens in May, where garlands are offered for sale and there is a grand parade of beautifully decorated floats. Later in the same month, at Trikeri, local girls perform folk dances in a rural setting, and those amongst them who are engaged decorate the doors of their fiancé's houses with wild flowers.

But one of the most unusual ceremonies which takes place in Greece, once the home of the mythical gods and goddesses of Mount Olympus, is when the Olympic flame is lit at ancient Olympia in the Western Peloponnese. This ceremony, in which a number of young maidens dressed in classical Greek robes take part, recreates the rite which preceded the first Olympic Games when they were first held, over three thousand years ago.

One of the girls, the High Priestess, kindles the flame by reflecting the sun's rays into an ancient bowl, and this flame is used to light the torch, which is carried by a series of runners to the site of the Olympic Games.

IT'S MINSTREL TIME

The Television Toppers at work.

How many girls have watched a lavish and spectacular show on stage or television and dreamed of becoming one of those glamorous dancing girls? A great many, judging by the number of girls who turn up for auditions to join the famous Television Toppers of "Black and White Minstrel" fame.

The glitter and sparkle of the lavish costumes worn by the Toppers in the highly successful Black and White Minstrel Show seem to act as a magnet to these girls, with the added promise of excitement and romance spurring them on to apply for auditions. But just what does it take to become a Television Topper?

First and foremost a girl must measure up to the physical requirements. She must have a good figure, be fairly tall and, of course, must have a good knowledge of dancing. The most essential attribute is fitness for, with twelve performances to be danced through each week, standards are exceptionally high. The youthful Toppers—average age seventeen to twenty-three—dance the equivalent of six-and-a-half miles each night! It's worth remembering that for each girl who gets into the chorus line, some three hundred are turned down.

But it's not all hard work; the girls do have a tremendous amount of fun and, of course, romances are inevitable. A staggering total of seventeen marriages have taken place between Toppers and Minstrel men since the show first started, and every year brings new romances and further marriages.

There is always the chance that some new and exciting opportunity may come along—like becoming a member of the Black and White Minstrel Show that tours in such countries as Australia and New Zealand or, of course, a chance to appear on television.

Every girl in the Toppers has an extensive wardrobe, including costumes which cost over £60 each, and twelve pairs of shoes. Feather fans can cost anything up to £80 and the elaborate headgear and jewellery would make a duchess go green with envy!

YOU HAVE TO BE FIT

A girl who knows quite a bit about life in the Toppers is Elspeth Hands, who joined the chorus-line eight years ago, when she was sixteen, and is now head dancer and assistant choreo-grapher at the Victoria Palace, London.

"I always wanted to dance," says Elspeth, "and when I left the Aida Foster School I spent a year as a Bluebell Girl. When I joined the Minstrels I was the 'baby' in the Toppers; now I'm the only one of the original dancers left in the company.

"I really enjoy my life with the Toppers, mainly because everyone is so happy and friendly. But I don't think I will go on dancing till I'm thirty; I want to concentrate more on the choreography side.

"All the girls in the company are extremely fit, as they need to be with eighteen costume changes every night, which necessitates racing twenty times up and down the thirty-two stairs between stage and dressing-room!

"Things do go wrong on occasions, of course. I remember one girl's hairpiece coming off and flying over the footlights into the orchestra pit!

"On another occasion we had a new dancer who was a little too enthusiastic. On her first night, and right in the middle of the opening number, she fell off stage into the orchestra pit!

"And, as if that wasn't funny enough, one of the male singers leapt forward and shouted: 'Don't worry, love.' And then he jumped into the orchestra pit after her!"

Robert Luff, the man who staged the Black and White Minstrel Show for the first time in 1960, took it to the Victoria Palace in 1962 for a few weeks' run. It remained there for seven years and was seen by more than five-and-a-half million people during 4,354 performances! It seemed an almost impossible task to better or even equal this success. Yet another Minstrel spectacular, called "The Magic of the Minstrels", opened at the Victoria Palace in November 1969, and in its first year alone was seen by almost one million people!

THE MAGIC OF THE MINSTRELS

"It's been fantastic playing before so many people," says attractive Scottish singing star, Margaret Savage, the show's leading lady. "In fact, even though I've been in the business for quite a few years, the response of a live audience still thrills me to bits."

Margaret's singing career spans some nine years, and a sizeable chunk of her time has been spent with the Black and White Minstrels, both on television and on the stage.

"There isn't another show quite like

Dorothy Ogden is the leading singer with the touring version of the Black and White Minstrel Show.

Elspeth Hands joined the Toppers when she was sixteen years old.

the Minstrels," says Margaret. "The 'magic' doesn't only exist for audiences, it also exists for the people in the show. It's very hard to explain in cold print. But I would say that the Black and White Minstrel Show is the biggest and happiest family of entertainers in the world today."

Apart from the Victoria Palace show there is always a Black and White Minstrel Show on tour. During 1971, girls in the touring show spent seasons in Manchester, Nottingham, Eastbourne and Bristol.

Small wonder, then, that during the ten-year existence of the Minstrel "factory", the Toppers have worn out thousands of pairs of fishnet tights, shoes, costumes, fans and headgear. And because of the vast amount of scenery and costumes, a special warehouse has been made out of a disused church in South London. It's a modern Aladdin's Cave!

BEHIND THE SCENES

There's a workroom with a couturier and six machinists, whose job it is to repair and alter the elaborate costumes. There is even a row of automatic washing machines, which churn out the laundry for the show at a cost of some £6,000 a year!

It may sound an exciting and glamorous job looking after all the costumes, jewellery and other material used in the show, but wardrobe supervisor Marie Worth has to work very hard to keep such a huge production immaculately dressed. Part of her job is knowing the exact measurements of every single girl and boy in the company, so that clothes can be kept intact and ready to wear at a minute's notice.

The laundering is a full-time job in itself, with 150 shirts per week—this is for one show only—and the same number of gloves, collars and briefs. In addition every girl in the show has at least nine costumes to wear during each performance!

Every girl in the Toppers has eight pairs of court shoes, dyed in different colours, and in addition they have gold and silver boots—a grand total of twelve pairs of shoes per girl.

Add to this the dyeing of costumes and storage of necklaces and headgear, and one begins to see the enormity of the task which has to be tackled by Marie Worth and her team.

When you become a Television Topper you're part of an extraordinary team; a team that tries to present some of the finest entertainment ever seen, and in which the glamorous Television Toppers play such an important part.

PIGGY POUFFE

designed by Katherine McLean.

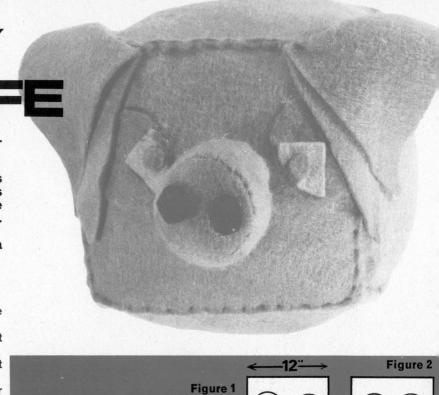

You've heard of piggy banks and piggy-back rides, but here's something new—a piggy pouffe that's quick and simple to make.

These instructions are for a 12×12×12 in. pouffe

MATERIALS:

Seven 12 in. squares of pink felt,
Two 3 in. diameter circles of purple felt for the eyes.
One 3 in. diameter circle of orange felt for the nose.
One 3 in. diameter circle of orange felt for the tail.
One 11×1½ in. strip of pink felt for the outside of the nose.
Scraps for the nostrils and the pupils.
Kapok or pieces of clean nylon stocking for stuffing.
One piece of 11¾×11¾ in. strong cardboard for the base.

First of all take one of your pink squares and glue the two purple eyes in place. When these have dried, glue on two smaller circles to make the pupils.

Figure 1

Now for the nose. Take the 3 in. circle of orange felt and stick two tiny nostrils to it. Then, with the nostrils inside, sew the pink strip neatly around the nose circle, and then turn it inside-out, so that the stitches are inside and the nostrils are outside. Now stuff the nose tightly, and position it on your face square. Using very tiny stitches, and sewing from the inside of the face, sew the nose to the face.

Figure 2

Now begin to sew the six squares together, leaving the seventh to form the ears. Sew with neat, small stitches on the inside, leaving the bottom edge of the back square open. Now turn inside-out, so that all your stitches are inside the cube shape. Slip the piece of cardboard into the opening to make a firm base, stuff the whole cube tightly, and sew the remaining seam neatly.

Figure 3

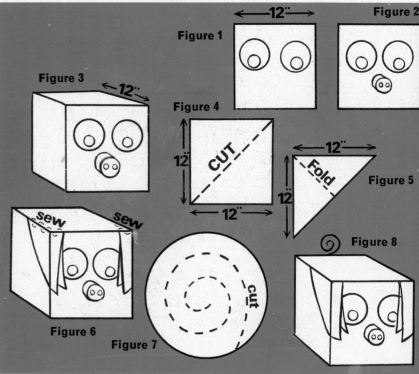

Figure 1 · Figure 2 · Figure 3 · Figure 4 · Figure 5 · Figure 6 · Figure 7 · Figure 8

The next things to make are the ears. Fold the remaining piece of pink felt in half along the diagonal, and cut.

Figure 4

Fold these two pieces again until you have smaller triangular shapes.

Figure 5

Sew these in place along the two top side seams, so that the eyes are covered slightly by the floppy ears.

Figure 6

Take your second circle of orange felt and cut out a curly tail, as in the diagram.

Figure 7

Sew this on to the top back seam, and your pouffe is finished.

Figure 8

Now all you have to do is to sit on it; after all that hard work you've earned yourself a rest!

MARI'S SECRET

*A story from
Welsh history
by Catherine Morris*

Mari sat spinning in the shadow of a boulder on the hillside as she watched the small flock of sheep that grazed on the slopes. Sheep were important to the Welsh peasantry of the early fifteenth century. Mutton fed the hungry, and fleeces became garments. Careful housewives sent the children to pluck strands of wool left by the sheep on gorse bushes and brambles. Such scraps of wool were spun into yarn. No girl was ever idle who was old enough to use the distaff.

So Mari spun, and as she spun she sang sweetly—a song about the greatness of the princes of Wales who had fought bravely and had lost, and died, but who would return again to lead Wales to victory.

Her song and her spinning lost their rhythm as the wool caught on a large wart on her hand. She stared at the ugly roughness, and muttered crossly.

"Mari, Mari, talking to yourself, and looking like a storm-cloud on the Mawddwy mountain. Shame on you

on such a fine day."

Mari looked up at Dafydd, the blacksmith's son, who grinned mockingly down at her.

"You it is then, Dafydd Ddu, and why are you not at your anvil on this fine day? Or did some great horse kick you up the mountain when you tried to shoe him?"

"What ails you, Mari? You of the sweet voice who puts the music of the harp to shame. Is it that wart on your finger. Come, I will take you to the Wise Woman who lives beside the Dyfi river. She will charm it away."

"But she is a witch!" exclaimed Mari in horror. "She casts spells, and sees dreadful things before they happen—like her mother and her grandmother before her."

Mari crossed herself as she whispered, "They say her grandmother foretold the death of Prince Llewellyn, our last prince, in a field of broom."

Dafydd, who had thrown himself on the short grass beside Mari, roared with laughter.

"Old wives' tales," he spluttered. "The Wise Woman is no witch. She has no evil eye. She makes good potions to cure a sick horse, or to ease aching bones. Come! Or are you afraid, Mari? You boast that no

mountain wolf dare come near your sheep while you watch, and now you fear an old woman with a crooked back."

"I am not afraid," cried Mari angrily. "I will come now, and if a wolf does devour my sheep you will have to reckon with my father's wrath."

And so, with Dafydd beside her, she strode angrily down the hillside, down through the oak forest, and down to the Dyfi stream that here began its flow to the waters of Cardigan Bay. The stream flowed silently under the shadow of the great oaks. There was a green stillness. Even the light seemed green, thought Mari, as she followed Dafydd through the thickets of hazels.

"Green is the colour of the fairies— the Fair Ones," muttered Mari. "It is a bad colour for mortals."

Step by step Mari's spurt of bravado slipped away. But she dared not tell Dafydd her fears. So, hiding her terror, she said loudly, "Where is this Wise Woman of yours? Does she hide like a toad under a stone?"

Dafydd put his hand firmly on Mari's mouth. "Mock not," he

hissed, "if you want to be rid of that wart."

Mari shivered. Meekly and silently she followed Dafydd to a rough hut made of wattles, which clung to a rock beside a deep pool. Beside the hovel sat an old crone stripping leaves from some herb, and laying them on a flat stone. As she worked, the Wise Woman chanted to herself.

Even when Mari and Dafydd stood before her, the hunchback droned on: "Beware, Glyndwr, Lord of the Glen of the Sacred Waters! Beware! The star that rose at your beginning is dimming. Yet you will live on with the magic of Arthur's sword, and the courage of Snowdonia's princes. Still will you make those Saxons in High Places tremble. Lords from afar will flock to your banner, and strange Kings befriend you. But your star falls, and bitterness will be our lot. Unknown will be your dwelling, and unknown your end."

The droning stopped. Sighing, the old woman said, "And now all is dark. I see no more."

Blinking, as if awaking from a deep sleep, the Wise Woman looked

up at Mari and Dafydd. Even Dafydd's smile was trembling, and Mari's legs felt useless as Dafydd thrust her forward on her knees before the Wise Woman.

Kneeling beside Mari, Dafydd said, "I am . . ."

Baring her gums in a welcoming grimace the crone interrupted: "You are Dafydd Ddu—so well named Dafydd the Dark-haired One. Is it a lame horse? Or has the maid lost her sheep on the mountain?"

"You know I watch the sheep?" asked Mari, trembling.

"I know many things. Too many sorrows for one woman to feel." The old eyes stared at Mari. "It is a wart, is it not? You want me to charm away that great wart that worries your spinning. Give me your hand, child, and stop shaking. Hungry I may be, but I do not eat children."

Willing her hand to keep still, Mari placed it in the old twisted hand.

"Get me a wet pebble from the river," the Wise Woman commanded Dafydd.

She accepted the wet pebble like a queen receiving homage, and rubbed it lightly on the ugly wart, muttering quietly to herself. Seven times it touched the wart from left to right, and seven times from right to left.

" 'Tis done," she said, nodding. "In seven days your hand will be clear of evil. But wrap your hand in a piece of red flannel."

"Thank you," whispered Mari. "I will bring you some ewe's milk tomorrow."

"I ask no payment," said the old woman. "But it is a kind thought." She paused, staring at Mari. The old eyes became vacant. She muttered, as if to herself, "One day, a misty day, you will give kindness and shelter to one without shelter. You will keep his secret from friends and enemies."

Her eyes cleared, and briskly she waved them away.

"Peace go with you," was the Wise Woman's blessing.

Mari cast a furtive, backward glance at the sitting figure. The Wise One was staring after them with tears flowing down her wrinkled face.

Silently, Dafydd and Mari pushed their way through the hazels.

Suddenly Dafydd stopped and, blushing, said, "You are the brave one, Mari. No other girl would have faced a meeting with the Wise Woman. I thought you would have run away 'ere we reached the river."

"She is unhappy, that one," said Mari slowly, "and not for herself. What did she mean when she said I would shelter somebody and keep it secret? It is our custom to help travellers. But I felt she meant no ordinary wayfarer. Cold fingers ran down my back as she spoke."

Dafydd shrugged. But he did not mock. "Who knows what she means when she talks to herself like somebody asleep. I think her mind was wandering," he concluded cheerfully. "Old folk's minds do wander."

"Maybe," said Mari quietly. "But

not *her* mind. She is not like other old ones."

Next morning, when Mari had counted her sheep and milked the ewes, she filled a pitcher with some milk and made her way down to the Wise Woman's hut. In the early morning light the scene was as eerie as it had been the previous afternoon. There was no sign of the crone, so Mari set the ewer on the flat stone, while a raven croaked dismally from a nearby crag.

On the seventh day after the Old One had charmed Mari's wart, the girl woke, feeling excited. Today would test the Wise Woman's powers. Slowly she unwound the soiled red flannel, and she exclaimed with joy when she saw her hand smooth and soft, without the slightest blemish. Mari marvelled as she washed her hands. Yet she felt scared. For the first time she had experienced something she couldn't understand.

"A witch," she whispered. Adding hastily, "A good witch."

Deciding that Dafydd must be told that the charm had worked, Mari left her sheep in the care of her younger sister, and ran down to the village, to the blacksmith's forge.

In the gloom, lit only by a roaring fire and the sparks from the anvil as Dafydd's father, Ifan, struck a red-hot ploughshare, Mari could not see Dafydd. Then she felt a tug on her arm, and Dafydd led her outside into the cool air.

"I have tidings. Fine tidings!" he exclaimed.

"I have something to show you," replied Mari, thrusting her hand at Dafydd.

"Oh, yes," he remarked lightly, "the wart is gone. I told you so. But listen. This is important."

Hurt at Dafydd's lack of interest, Mari muttered, "Just like a boy! Only his silly games matter."

Dafydd's eyes shone with excitement as he said, "Owain Glyndwr, whose coming was heralded by a great star, comes to Machynlleth. He is to give us a Parliament, and we will be ruled again by a prince of our blood. He has taken castle after castle, and outfought the Saxon king, and the kings of France and Scotland

are his friends. Is it not good to live in such stirring times, Mari?"

"The Wise Woman spoke of him," said Mari in a startled voice. "We did not understand. You thought her mind was wandering. But she said too that Glyndwr's star will fall. He will vanish from the eyes of men."

"The old dame babbles in her sleep," retorted Dafydd hotly. "She had heard of the star, and the rest is foolish talk."

"But how would she know about the star, and the lords from far-

away, and the kings? Nobody would talk to her of such things. *I* knew not, nor *you*, till this day."

"Even if I did not know," said Dafydd crossly, "tomorrow I go to Machynlleth to help my uncle shoe the horses of Glyndwr's army. If you so wish, you may ride pillion with me on my pony."

"I have never been in a town, not even on market day," said Mari. "I might even see the prince. We must leave early in the morning. It is all of ten miles."

"When dawn breaks we must away," warned Dafydd. "It will be rough riding, with many streams to cross."

That night Mari was too excited to sleep. Before dawn she dressed in her Sunday best, wearing four flannel petticoats and her mother's best shawl, which had belonged to Mari's great-grandmother.

Even the sheep were huddled in sleep when Mari left the hillside cottage and walked down to the village, which she reached as the first grey streaks showed the approach of dawn.

Dafydd's sturdy mountain pony stood outside the forge. Dafydd was filling the side-panniers on the pony when Mari joined him. She stared at the loaded creature.

"Do we walk then?" she asked.

"The poor dumb animal cannot carry those baskets and both of us."

"This is a pony, not a sheep," snapped Dafydd. "He will carry us well enough."

"I brought some bakestone bread and ewe cheese," remarked Mari, nervously. Dafydd, she thought, was in a strange mood.

"Good. I have bread and boiled bacon. Put yours in the left-hand-side pannier with mine."

"What is in the other pannier?" asked Mari.

"My leather apron, and things I shall need," replied Dafydd evasively. "One more thing. Then we must start."

Dafydd led the loaded pony to the mounting-stones used by riders. Mari settled herself on the pony, sitting side-saddle, and arranging her petti-

coats as fine as any great lady. Then, to her amazement, Dafydd handed her his great bow.

"Hold this while I mount," he said quietly.

He watched the forge door anxiously. Obediently, Mari took the bow. The quiver and the arrows, she suddenly realised, must be in the pannier with Dafydd's leather apron. Saying nothing, she handed him the bow when he had mounted—dodging the weapon as Dafydd put it over his head and rested it on his back.

Nobody came to the forge door to bid them good-bye. And when they left the village, having met no living creature except a bad-tempered dog, Dafydd gave a sigh of relief.

"Is it your father's bow?" asked Mari, mischievously. "Is that why

you watched the door, fearing he would come out to claim it?"

" 'Tis the family bow," replied Dafydd stiffly. "You are a good rider, are you not, Mari?"

"What mountain girl is not?" remarked Mari.

"True. You can take the pony back this evening."

"But . . ." began Mari.

"I am going with Glyndwr's army," said Dafydd quietly. "Wales needs every archer Glyndwr can muster. And a good blacksmith can always be useful. Father needs the pony. I knew you would take it back for me."

"You could have told me that it was a servant you wanted, not a companion," cried Mari indignantly. "You are deep and cunning, Dafydd Ddu."

Dafydd chuckled.

"One good turn deserves another. Who took you to the Wise Woman, and rid you of that plaguey wart?"

The Wise Woman! Mari seemed to see her, and to hear her chant: "But your star falls, and bitterness will be our lot."

"Do not go, Dafydd," begged Mari. "The rebellion will fail."

"Glyndwr's fight is our fight," proclaimed Dafydd, "and I will not heed womanish talk."

It took several hours for the little pony to cover the ten miles of hills and heath, to cross precipitous valleys and fast-running streams. But at last the riders saw the smoke rising from distant, wide chimneys, and presently the smell of wood smoke welcomed them.

Mari had not formed any picture of Machynlleth. On the outskirts were clusters of humble, small wattle and mud houses. But, as they progressed, more prosperous houses appeared; some built of roughly hewn stone. Here country folk sat at the roadside selling their wares, though little trade was done. The crowd of yeomen farmers with their labourers, and the wool merchants with their apprentices, awaited the coming of Owain Glyndwr, once Squire of Glyndwfrdwy, now acknowledged by France and Scotland and the Welsh people as the Prince of Wales.

In his anxiety not to miss seeing the hero, Dafydd forgot Mari, which suited her well, because from the back of the pony she could see over the heads of the people standing in front of her.

Suddenly the crowd stopped babbling. A great silence fell upon them. Some in the front fell on their knees, crossed themselves and prayed for the deliverance of Owain Glyndwr and their country. A small body of archers and spearmen marched proudly before the white banner with the golden dragon of Glyndwr.

The Prince sat well on his horse. His face was that of a thinker and a scholar, rather than that of a tough warrior.

Mari stared her fill, and her heart was filled with sorrow remembering the tragic words of the Wise Woman: "Your star is falling. . . . Unknown will be your dwelling, and unknown your end."

Somewhere, a harp played softly, and a bard sang a resounding martial song. So Glyndwr, dreamer and warrior, entered the hall to bestow on his people their first and only Parliament.

"A face I shall never forget," whispered Mari to herself.

friend to the house. Your aunt will be glad of her company. This is no place for a young girl, or an old one either."

In the stable Mari said, "I will get the pony hay and water, and rub him down. Will I see you again, Dafydd?" Filling a hide-bucket from a water-trough, she said, "Perhaps there is no place for you with Glyndwr."

Dafydd lowered his voice, saying, "Keep a secret, Mari. I am not seeking a place. I shall just take my bow and my arrows, and find myself a spear, and join the foot-soldiers. Nobody will notice an extra face."

"So I needs must wish you God speed now," said Mari. "I had best return in two hours. 'Tis not a journey I would welcome in the darkness."

"Speak to my father," said Dafydd. "He will understand. May the Holy Virgin protect you, Mari."

Without more ado, Dafydd left Mari. She never saw him again.

Having spent a few hours with the smith's wife, Mari felt refreshed, and she thought the pony would be fresh enough to make the ten-mile trek uphill to the hamlet which had been Dafydd's home.

She dreaded the journey. But even more than the journey she dreaded telling Dafydd's father that his only son, his sole helper at the forge, had gone to join Glyndwr's forays, which could take him anywhere in North and South Wales, and over the border into the dangerous Marcher lands of the English barons.

The return journey proved easier than Mari expected. The pony, lighter by two panniers and a heavy country boy, and probably sensing that the end of the task would mean the comfort of his home ground, carried Mari with a will.

Even the feared encounter with Dafydd's father passed peaceably. As soon as he heard the pony's hoof-beats, the smith left the forge to greet Mari.

"You ride well," he said. "I knew my son would not take my only pony."

"But . . ." began Mari, moistening her dry lips.

The smith raised his hand, and

"Wake up, Mari girl," cried Dafydd, tugging at her skirt. "Sitting up there like a queen. Why didn't you get down?"

"You forgot to help me down," retorted Mari smartly.

"So I did," grinned Dafydd. "Now you had better stay there and take care of the panniers. I shall have to lead the pony to my uncle's forge. I cannot ride in this crowd."

As they wove their way through the excited throng Mari saw nobody. She saw only in her mind's eye the face of Owain Glyndwr, and she shivered.

"There will be foot-soldiers needing weapons sharpened or repaired, and horsemen bringing their war horses for shoeing at my uncle's," yelled Dafydd above the noise of the crowd. "So I am sure to learn how to join Glyndwr."

Mari made no response, and Dafydd expected none.

As Dafydd had expected, there were soldiers inside and outside the forge. Never had his uncle been so busy. His face, blackened by the smoke of the forge, split into a grin when he saw Dafydd.

"Praise be to the Saints, help has come!" he exclaimed. "Stable your pony at the back, boy, and take your

103

Mari flinched. Surely he would not strike her. But it was simply a gesture conveying a request for silence.

"Say no more, Mari. The Wise Woman called a scant hour after you left. She told me Dafydd would never return from Glyndwr's wars." The smith shrugged his huge shoulders. "It is only right. Glyndwr is the hope of Wales. My grandfather died with our last Prince—Llewellyn ap Gruffydd. His great-grandson follows Glyndwr, to what end I know not, though the Wise Woman says . . ."

Dumbly, Mari nodded. She knew too well what the old woman with the wild blue eyes said. Bidding the smith farewell, Mari slowly climbed the hill she had descended so gaily before dawn. It seemed years, not hours, since then.

Months passed. Occasionally a pedlar, or a Welshman returning from the wars, brought scraps of news of the troubled world beyond the hills. 'Twas said that Owain Glyndwr took castles in the Marches, and when Henry the Fourth or his young son, already a formidable leader, retook them, Glyndwr and his men won them again.

Like a will-o'-the-wisp, Glyndwr led his men hither and thither. He was said to possess magical qualities.

Then came the hardest winter Wales had ever known in living memory. The whole world seemed frozen. The birds died in their thousands, till there were no birds left. And there was no more news. No huckster cried his wares in the countryside. No ragged warrior crossed the snowbound hills.

After some weeks of snow and ice, Mari wondered how the Wise Woman was faring down by the river. Taking a hunk of boiled bacon and some rye bread she struggled through the snow to the old woman's hut. But when she got there she was afraid to enter lest the Ancient was dead.

But before she knocked a voice called, "Enter, Mari."

When Mari entered into the gloom, lit only by a peat fire, the Wise Woman said, "I knew you would come. It is your destiny to succour the helpless and the vanquished."

Mari passed over the bacon and the rye-bread and said, "I feared you would be sick or . . ."

The hunchback chuckled. "Or dead. Like the birds. No, I live, and my raven lives too, on the crag."

She stirred the smouldering fire under the big pot that hung from a chain.

"You bring me good food, and all I can offer you is a drink made of dried nettles. But 'tis hot and health-giving."

Touched, Mari accepted the warming drink gratefully.

Suddenly the old woman said quietly: "The star is fallen. The golden dragon tarnished. Where the star fell and where the golden dragon lies, nobody knows. Wales did not win her freedom."

"But there is no news," whispered Mari.

The Wise Woman stared into the fire, and made no answer. And, after a while, Mari left, wondering and fearing.

The cold snap passed, and then came rain and mists, and with them the sad tidings that Glyndwr was defeated, and had vanished.

Mari had lost some sheep in snowdrifts. Now she tried to keep track of the remainder in the mists. As she searched the hillside for them on a particularly wet and misty day, Mari suddenly came up against a figure in the mist. She uttered a startled cry.

"Fear not, child," said a quiet voice. "I am only a wanderer, lost in my country's hills."

The mist which, as mists do, made the figure seem gigantic, suddenly thinned, and Mari, with a little gasp, saw the man's face—the face of the great leader she had seen ride with his white banner and golden dragon when he gave Wales a Parliament—the face of Owain Glyndwr.

Mari tried to kneel. "Sir," she whispered.

"Nay, child. Kneel not to an unknown wayfarer who takes his rest in caves."

"Sir," whispered Mari, "I have a hut I use during lambing. 'Tis but humble, but it is dry and warm, and has a store of salted meats and rye-bread, and you can get water from a brook."

"And you would bestow this on a stranger for a brief time, and then forget him?"

Mari replied earnestly, "I would, in gratitude, and forget I had met him. But forget him? Never. And neither will his countrymen. The hut lies this way."

As Mari led Owain Glyndwr to his sanctuary she suddenly remembered the Wise Woman's words at their first meeting: "One misty day, you will give kindness and shelter to one without shelter. You will keep his secret." And, later, "It is your destiny to succour the helpless and the vanquished."

When the spring sunshine bathed the hillside, Mari visited the hut. It was empty.

The country folk whispered that Owain Glyndwr was here, or there. But nobody knew where. Mari, listening to their gossip, smiled quietly to herself, and kept her secret.

Music is one of the greatest forms of art, and the famous musicians of the past left us a rich heritage which we can all enjoy today. But they were also mortal men with a fair share of joys and sorrows during their lifetime, some of which can be heard in their music by those who have heart enough to hear.

ROBERT ALEXANDER SCHUMANN (1810–1856)

When Robert Schumann gave up the law to study under a very harsh music master named Wieck, he gained not only a wealth of musical knowledge but also a lovely and talented bride, for he fell in love with Clara Wieck, his tutor's young daughter. But her father opposed the marriage—he even tore up one of Schumann's best compositions in a fit of rage—and the young couple were forced to go to the courts for permission to marry. Clara was an inspiration to her husband, who gave the world such wonderful works as the *Spring Symphony*, and although Schumann suffered a severe mental breakdown and Clara outlived him by some forty years, the marriage was extremely happy.

JOHANN SEBASTIAN BACH (1685–1750)

Another composer who worked late into the night was young Johann Sebastian Bach, who secretly copied out the works of great composers by candlelight from the original manuscripts which were the cherished possessions of his elder brother.

Johann had a fine singing voice and this gained him a place at a famous choir school in Luneburg. While he was there Johann often walked many miles to hear great organists play. Returning from one such concert he stopped, tired and hungry, outside a wayside inn. A moment later two herring heads fell at his feet and, as he picked them up, Johann saw to his astonishment that they contained two golden coins.

The kind-hearted traveller who had chosen this amusing way of helping a weary boy probably never knew that he had given the coins to someone who was destined to become the composer of some of the best organ music ever to be played.

FRANZ SCHUBERT (1797–1828)

At seventeen, Schubert was a schoolmaster, often writing musical notes at the bottom of a pupil's book instead of remarks about his work, and dreaming of the day when he would become a famous composer. Franz had been able to practise every day because a young apprentice had shown him a secret store of pianos in a nearby warehouse, and Franz had been able to choose any he wished.

Although people dubbed him "Fat Franz", they always begged him to play for their dances. Franz also composed many lovely songs such as *Who is Sylvia?* and *Hedge Roses*.